Triples, Trios, and Triads

By Ronald J. Cohn

Triples, Trios, and Triads

An Eclectic Journey

By
Ronald J. Cohn

ISBN Number

ISBN 978-1-7348902-0-4

9 781734 890204

90000>

Typeface

Book Antiqua

Snakeonrope Press

For my wife Carol
who has put up with me while this book came into focus.

Acknowledgments

Very special thanks to Ellen Sorbone for viewing the manuscript with a critical eye and for making many valued suggestions on technical, structural, and philosophical issues. The manuscript would never have reached a professional level but for her help and diligent work. Thanks also to Diane Beeson for pointing out an excursion I didn't have to take. Thanks to Roberto Loiederman for taking a look at the manuscript. Thanks to Lola Popkin for showing me sources of copyright free photos she learned about in her sixth-grade media studies course.

The mistakes that remain are all mine.

And special thanks to the Universe who has been letting the bubble that is the author of this book float around all this time

Introduction

Guruji was leading a small group of pilgrims up a long hill in the Himalayas near the Ganges River. He was regal. He wore nothing but a white loincloth. His long white hair fluttered, and his long white beard bounced along with his gait. As we passed him, we heard his sermon. "Brahma created this world; Shiva is destroying this world; but there is no need to worry, for Vishnu is sustaining the world, instant by instant."

Triads, trios, and triples have been around for a long time. A triad, I learned in school, is the pre-modern, the modern, and the post-modern, but it is obsolete now as we've moved from the pre-digital age to the digital age.

A phrase by the theologian Abraham Joshua Heschel that hasn't left my mind for many years is, "Wonder, Awe, and Radical Amazement." What are my grandkids to make of this when "awe" has been conflated with "cool" and you can buy awesome things and experiences? They say to me, "Oh you're so nineteen hundreds!"

Here's a triad from the Celtic wisdom tradition that will never become obsolete - three types of men who do not understand women are: young men, middle-aged men, and old men.

But wait a second, hold up! Yuval Harari told the world leaders at Davos in 2018 that we might be one of the last generations of homo sapiens and within a century or two, the earth will be dominated by entities as different from us as we are from Neanderthals and chimpanzees because of advances in:

- The engineering of bodies
- The engineering of brains
- The engineering of minds.

What will become of the sexes of our species then? Will there be any difference? Will there only be two?

This book is a mélange of the profound and the mundane. You will find in these pages triples, trios, and triads like Rumsfeld-Cheney-Bush, the three stooges Curly-Mo-Larry, Copernicus-Descartes-Kant, Tin man-Scarecrow-Lion from the wizard of Oz, knower-knowing-known, the Nat King Cole Trio from the 1940s and 1950s, and solid-liquid-gas.

How and why I picked the "threes" I did comes from my personal journey. I'm a guy from the 20th century who retired back to the Bay Area in 2004. I was here in the late 1960s. I get my information these days, in this wonderful blue state bubble, from reading the New York Times and from my subscriptions to the New York Review of Books and Scientific American. I listen to the local Pacifica radio station, KPFA. I read books on science, eastern spirituality, and history. As my mind hunts and gathers, other miscellaneous streams of content also flow into my consciousness.

I started collecting these tidbits in the 1970s. Themes you will find as you amble through the collection, grown now to over 500 entries, are *Advaita* philosophy, American history and politics, Buddhist ideas, Celtic triads, deep culture, European history, Indian Vedanta philosophy, music, pop culture, religion, science, Western Philosophy, and gleanings from the wisdom traditions.

Just the other day, I saw this quote from Shakespeare chiseled on a wooden panel hanging on a friend's dining room wall:

> *Love all,*
> *Trust a few,*
> *Do wrong to none.*

How to Experience This Book

This is not a book to be read continuously. Take your time with the collection. Meander, ponder, consider, contemplate, meditate, laugh, and enjoy. I mean it! Think of this book as a long piece of music in which each triad is a chord. The various bits are spread out in time and space; they are not lumped together into subject category-boxes such as finance, history, and science.

The beat goes on. It's a waltz. Bits like "the three blind mice" or "the three stooges" keep the beat. A bit like Harari's "Evolution of economies from Feudalism to Capitalism to Dataism" requires a pause and some thought. A bit from the teachings of French Oneness teacher, Jean Klein, "He who is knowingly aware is simultaneously:

- Living witness
- Audience
- Actor

of the perceptions" requires the beat to pause as we contemplate or meditate on Klein's meaning.

Each page of this book takes up a separate page spread. Take your time. The graphics also keep the beat. And keep in mind the quote below.

Ron Cohn March 2019

> *This world of…triads appears only in the mind*
> *like the illusory ring of fire*
> *formed in darkness*
> *by whirling the point of a glowing rope-end.*

—Sri Muruganar, disciple of Ramana Maharshi

Three bets pay money at the horse races:
- Win
- Place
- Show

A ramblin' cowboy once said, " Gimme
- A young horse
- Old whiskey
- Fast women

The Marine Corps' concepts of:
- Mind
- Body
- Spirit

sold on TV to would-be recruits and three concepts used, as well, by the wisdom teachers exhorting us to merge them into a harmonious Unity of Being.

The Hindu:
- Brahma the creator
- Vishnu the sustainer
- Shiva the destroyer.

Reinhold Niebuhr's famous Serenity Prayer; Grant me:
- Serenity to accept the things I cannot change
- Courage to change the things I can
- Wisdom to know the difference."

The three medieval worlds of Dante:
- Heaven
- Purgatory
- Hell.

The Christian trinity:
- Father
- Son
- Holy Ghost

Yuval Noah Harari lists three revolutions that shaped the course of history on the first page of his book, <u>Sapiens</u>:
- The Cognitive Revolution started up history about 70,000 years ago with the advent of learning, remembering, and communicating
- The Agricultural Revolution dawned 10,000 years ago
- The Scientific Revolution began 500 years ago. We're still immersed in it today. It may well end history and start something different. "We're in for quite a ride." said Harari. The soldiers and workers, being replaced by drones and robots, are not as important to the power elite as they were 100 years ago. Heath care disparities prove it. The rich live longer and healthier lives. Forget class differences if we evolve into different species.

Harari wrote that after the Cognitive Revolution, it was not enough to understand Homo sapiens through the interactions of:
- Genes
- Hormones
- Organisms.

but through the interactions of:
- Ideas
- Images
- Fantasies.

The three blind mice

A triad that is a unity:
- The doing
- The doer
- The deed

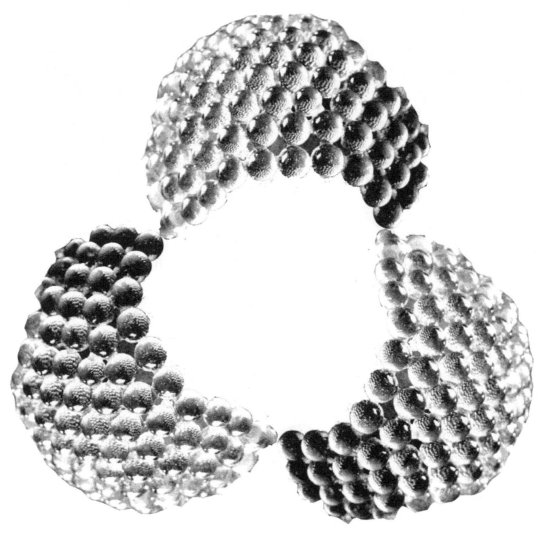

The three rungs on the ladder to Wisdom:
- Hearing the truth
- Pondering over it
- Merging with it in meditation.   from the Hindu Wisdom tradition

"Goldilocks and the Three Bears" is a fairy tale in which a little girl with a grand sense of entitlement breaks into a stranger's house and tries three of everything: bowls of porridge, chairs, and beds, and keeps trying until she finds things to be just right. When the bears come home, she runs away...

Why didn't the bears eat her up? When will the bears come home on the "Goldilocks" economy? Who are the bears in this metaphor? Investopedia says that a Goldilocks economy is one that is not so hot that it causes inflation, not so cold that it causes a recession, but just right so that the stock prices stay high.

Astronomers conceive of a Goldilocks region around the sun where it's not too hot and it's not too cold, but just right for a biology to evolve in four billion years that can feature both a Beethoven and an Auschwitz.

Cosmologists conceive of a Goldilocks universe in which the fundamental properties and parameters are just right for galaxies to form, for a sun to form that lasts long enough for life on one of its planets to evolve into a consciousness that asks questions about the universe. For this to happen, the strength of gravity, the masses of the electron and proton, the electric charge of the electron, the relative strengths of the gravitational and nuclear forces, the overall mass density of the universe as well as its rate of expansion all have to all be just right, not too big and not too small. For example, if gravity is too strong, the stars will be compressed into black holes before they can light up, but if the nuclear force is too strong, the stars will light up too fast and evolve to their deaths in millions of years instead of the billion years needed for a biology to evolve with conscious

humans.

The Caliph's Splendor, by Benson Bobrick, tells of a book written by a Syrian trader at the time when the Arabs ruled Sicily. The trader wrote that there are three kinds of merchants:
- "He who travels
- He who stocks
- He who exports."

furthermore, the trader noted, three ways for carrying out a transaction:
- Cash sale with a time limit for delivery
- Purchase on credit with installment payments
- Contracts for investments in trading ventures.

The Vedic prayer in which we ask the Divine to lead us:
- From untruth to truth
- From darkness to light
- From death to immortality.

Sigmund Freud's three concepts:
- Id
- Ego
- Superego.

According to his psychoanalytic theory, these three parts create the complex behavior of human beings. This material is from "A Psychological Analysis of Frankenstein by Mary Shelley" by Neha Vaz who gives these examples:
- Id: The Creature---The part of a person's unconscious mind that relates to basic needs and desires. A newborn child's actions are based on the id, and the child only develops an ego and superego as it grows up.
- Ego: The part of a person's mind that is responsible for dealing with reality. A large part of the ego's purpose is to delay the demands of the id until the appropriate time.
- Superego: The superego is morally perfect and is formed based on the morals and values that we have learned from our parents, and the ideas about right and wrong that we learn from society.

See https://prezi.com/aadnvntzis-d/a-psychological-analysis-of-frankenstein-by-mary-shelley/

A common statement of our wonderful freedom and equal opportunity occurring regardless of:
- Race
- Color
- Creed.

Arthur C. Brooks asked a swami in India, "...is economic prosperity a good or bad thing?" The answer was, "Yes, of course, it can cure hunger." Brooks is concerned about getting past the snares of materialism that inhibit a person's living a good and satisfactory life. He offers three suggestions:

- Collect experiences, not things
- Steer clear of excessive usefulness. Aristotle makes this point when he admires learned men---"they knew things that are remarkable, admirable, difficult, and divine, but useless"
- Get to the center of the wheel of fortune as it revolves round and round; for on the rim are the spinning rounds of health, wealth, reputation, and emotions, but at the still point of the center lies the eternal truth.
  see "Abundance Without Attachment" (NYT 12/12/2014)

"If a master mason you would be, observe you well the Rule of Three." (*This dictum is given at http://books.google.com/ in the Google digital library entry for the "Masonic Magazine" of 1882-1883.*)

G. I. Gurdjieff stated the rule as:

- Affirming force
- Denying force
- Reconciling force

A wisdom teaching says that people have three conceits, for their:

- Station of birth
- Wealth
- Learning.

The philosopher Hegel used the triadic formulation "thesis-antithesis-synthesis." An example is the French Revolution, the ensuing Reign of Terror, and their resolution in a constitutional state of free citizens.

Marx and Engles used dialectical materialism to work with the triad:

- Working Class
- Capitalist Class
- Communist Society.

P.D. Ouspensky wrote about his mentor Gurdjieff's teachings. The Law of Three is the Law of the Three Forces of Creation. Every manifestation in the universe is the combination of three forces:

- Active Force (1st force)
- Passive Force (2nd force)
- Neutralizing Force (3rd force).

I dunno 'bout this ... seems like a pair of rose-colored glasses that one can put on to intellectualize away anything you want to explain...like "God", "devil", "karma", or the origin and destination of evolution.

Every time the bureaucratic fan gets hit, we must have an inquiry that is:

- Independent
- Thorough
- Transparent.

In his book, Politics, Aristotle classified governments as:

- Rule by the One - monarchy
- Rule by the Few - aristocracy
- Rule by the Many - democracy.

The ancient governments are explained by Arthur Herman in his book, <u>The Cave and the Light.</u> Aristotle said that all three forms had their deficiencies and times of Development, Ascendency, and Decay. About the deficiencies, professor of history, Arthur Eckstein, said that each form has its shadow side:
- Monarchy's shadow side is tyranny
- Aristocracy's shadow side is oligarchy
- Democracy's shadow side is mob rule.
  (KPFA radio interview with Mitch Jezerich 10/17/2018)

Herman goes on to discuss a history of Rome by Polybius who saw that Rome contained characteristics of each form:
- Two consuls of the I*mperium*
- The Senate
- The assemblies of the *plebes* who chose the consuls

giving it strength, but also its fate to go through three historical stages.

"The appearance of U.S. Department of Defense visual information does not imply or constitute DOD endorsement."
Photo By: Lance Cpl. Megan Brown   https://media.defense.gov/2018/May/07/2001913533/-1/-1/0/180503-M-UI426-0755C.JPG

In <u>A Middle Way – The Secular/Spiritual Road to Wholeness,</u> Duke Robinson points out that with the rise of science, Europeans were realizing that the ancient worldview of Christendom no longer fit their universe and that the Church had led them not to paradise but to a prison of:
- Ignorance
- Error
- Fear

That world view, says Robinson, established by the heights of the Dark Ages was based on:

- Greek Dualism - God's truth resides in some Platonic *uberworld*
- Christian doctrine- God sent his only son down from that *uberworld*
- Roman concept of empire expressed as the Church's male hierarchy.

The types of science used in the great governmental efforts of the 20th century to produce weapons of mass destruction: (Bill Joy, *Wired Magazine 04/2000*)

- Nuclear
- Chemical
- Biological

Wikipedia notes that the visuals for the Blue Meanies were mostly designed by Heinz Edelmann

The fruits of 2400 years of Western civilization according to Arthur Herman:

- Reason
- Tolerance
- Individual Freedom

All were rejected, he says, by a generation of Germans and Austrians as they rounded up and persecuted "undesirables." Stalin in Russia, Mao in China, and people in subcultures in the USA and other "backward" parts of the world have also rejected this Aristotelian triad. The influence of the "Blue Meanies" is still so strong. What to do? Let us all call upon the spirit and music of Dr. Pepper and his Lonely-Hearts Club Band to lead us in the battle against the age-old scourge, the Blue Meanies led by their Philosopher Kings. See "The Yellow Submarine", a Beatles movie of 1968, in which the nice loving people were overrun by an army of ugly Blue Meanies who hated music, stomped on all the flowers, and made all the children as sad as when a yellow-haired "meany" took the children away from their parents in 2018 and put them in concentration camps.

Herman concludes his book with a paean to Ayn Rand as she extols the threefold Aristotelian virtues of American Capitalism:

- Free market productivity
- Science
- Technical engineers.

The leaders of the free market are its Randean heroes: the entrepreneurs, the one percenter "job creators", the CEOs, and board members of global corporations. These are the Blue Meanies sucking out profits. After WWII, they made 40 times the workers' pay. Now in the 21st century, they make 1000s of times the workers' pay. The enterprises of the Blue Meanies extract riches from the planet and its people. Their corporate investments poison nature with their effluvia and poison the body politic with their money. Doesn't Professor Herman realize that these Randean heroes are the Blue Meanies, the philosopher kings of the modern global corporation, whose warriors are the marketing and PR departments, and whose producers are non-unionized workers told to follow orders coming down the chain of command and induced, along with all the other citizens, to consume the products of stuff they produce?

Three aspects of our so-called real world, the:

- Measured
- Measurer
- Measuring process.

Quantum physicist, Marcelo Gleiser, writes, "There is a continuum extending from the object detected to the detector and, finally to the consciousness of the observer." His book is The Island of Knowledge. If we take the human body to be the detector, then this measuring-triple becomes "experienced, experiencer, and experiencing" which happens in, on, and within the background of our awareness. This awareness is who we really are says *advaita* teacher Rupert Spira. His book is Being Aware of Being Aware.

Three common phases of H$_2$O:
- Ice
- Water
- Steam.

When a system is presented with certain conditions of temperature and pressure, it undergoes a phase transition. The transition can start slowly with a few isolated bubbles and gradually the system comes to a rolling boil, or the transition can occur suddenly with the onset of snow or rain.

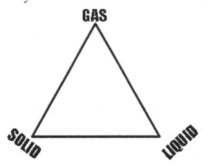

Ayn Rand's Aristotelian capitalism underwent a phase transition sometime after WWII with the growth of global corporations. The overarching philosopher kings of fascism and communism were defeated, but phoenix-like, they arose again in the disparate management structures of the global economy. Ayn Rand couldn't have seen how far we've come in the early 21st century:
- A national security state
- A vast inequality in the distribution of wealth
- A plethora of digital devices the citizens use to immerse themselves in a virtual reality playground that is mining them for personal data and that overlays their physical embeddedness with the trends of the day or the hour. Meanwhile the real world seems to be going to hell in a hand basket.

Here is a meme that came into my mind. Some of those elites played both sides in the great good vs. evil war of the 20th century. They even sought damages for their bombed-out facilities from the winners after the war.

A morning raga played on sitar, tambura, and tabla.

Historian of technology, George Dyson, said "digital universe" is not a metaphor for Apple gadgets and Google services, but a real aspect of the world created in the 1940s when numbers "no longer just stood for things but did things." Self-replicating and self-generating algorithms are at the cresting wave of evolution as they have been for four billion years, and now also as sentinels of technological evolution. The three players in the game of life and evolution he warns about in his book, <u>Darwin Among the Machines</u>, are:

- Human beings
- Nature
- Machines.

Dyson asks, "Could this be the end of the world as we know it if these self-replicating numerical creatures get loose?" He is a regular contributor to "edge.org" (https://www.edge.org/conversation/george_dyson-a-universe-of-self-replicating-code)

In "Who Are We " (NYT 2/17/16), Thomas Friedman lists the three greatest sources of America's strength:
• A culture of entrepreneurship
• An ethic of pluralism
• The quality of our governing institutions
But alas, during the election of 2016, he heard the leading candidates trashing all these strengths.

Three limitations of science:

- A person cannot make moral judgments based solely upon scientific findings.
- A person cannot make aesthetic judgments based solely upon scientific findings.
- Science cannot weigh in on
  - ➤ the Mystical
  - ➤ the Spiritual
  - ➤ the Supernatural

Science is limited because it is based upon measurements using the human senses or amplified extensions of those senses like microscopes, telescopes, precise laser beams, hadron super colliders, tuned electronic circuits, computerized statistics, or thought models in the mind. Galileo kept his finger on his pulse to measure time as he studied bodies in motion. Clocks are more accurate today by a factor of trillions, but they are still only counting beats.

The power of science lies in the fact that no priest, rabbi, or imam can counter its truths with appeals to religious dogma, scriptures, visions, or dreams. Science works on the hierarchy:

- Data
- Laws
- Theory.

Measurements are made. Regularities in the data are described by mathematical laws. Multiple laws are organized by a theory. In the history of science, we classically have:

- Danish astronomer, Tycho Brahe, (1546-1606) making precise observations of the motion of the planets with his naked eye in his observatory
- Johannes Kepler 1571-1630) organizing Brahe's data into three laws
- Isaac Newton (1642-1726) creating a universal theory of gravitation and motion to explain these laws.

Johannes Kepler's three laws of planetary motion:

- The orbit of a planet is an ellipse with the Sun at one of the two foci.
- A line segment joining a planet and the Sun sweeps out equal areas of the ellipse during equal intervals of time as it moves around the sun.
- The square of the orbital period of a planet is proportional to the cube of the semi-major axis of its elliptical orbit.

Kepler lived near the late 16th century to early 17th century's turbulent vortex of:

- War
- Religion
- Politics.

He kept his spirits and enthusiasm up by developing his medieval construction of the 5 Platonic solids, one embedded in the next to inform a nesting of six concentric spheres to provide a theoretical platform for the known planets of his time. He interrupted his work only to defend his imprisoned mother against charges of being a witch. (Frank Wilczek <u>A Beautiful Question</u>).

In the generation after Kepler, Newton devised a theory of motion composed of his three laws of classical mechanics plus his universal law of gravitation:

- Every object in a state of uniform motion tends to remain in that state of motion unless an external force is applied to it.
- The relationship between an object's mass (**m**), its acceleration (**a**), and the applied force (**F**), is **F = ma** (This is the law that Einstein improved upon by replacing **m** by a mass that gets bigger and bigger as the speed gets closer and closer to the speed of light. The energy trying to increase the speed is converted into mass instead of speed. You know, like **E=mc²**)
- For every action, there is an equal and opposite reaction.

Galileo Galilei, who died the year Newton was born, empirically established laws of motion that Newton explained by these three laws of motion.

The three dimensions of space which we learn about by the time we stand up in our crib:

- front-back **x**
- left-right **y**
- up-down **z**

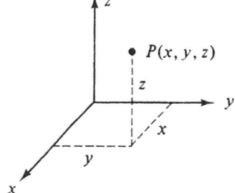

These are the Cartesian coordinates, a triple of numbers symbolized by the letters, x, y, and z, for every point in space. Digital computers and neuronal brains use these triples to internally represent a three-dimensional world. The Cartesian coordinate system represents geometry as pure "number." The math used for working out the details of Newton's Laws of motion is the calculus that Newton invented.

By the time we play games of in and out and all around in the kindergarten, we have another way to represent 3-D space. For example, erect a maypole on a flat playground, then the three dimensions of space can be represented by the different but equivalent set of numbers called polar coordinates:

- distance out from the base of the maypole
- angle going around the maypole
- angle lifting off the playground's surface

This set of coordinates (symbolized by the Greek letters: ρ, θ, φ), is good to use if you want to describe the position of a satellite, a ballistic missile, or a piece of space garbage. In this case, we have the distance of the object from the center of the earth, its longitude angle, and its latitude angle. Using these coordinates, A.I. computers could track every single object floating or flying out there. (I hope there're not tracking all the stuff going on in my mind).

The Newtonian Cartesians thought they had a neatly wrapped up clockwork world until Albert Einstein proclaimed, "It's not 3D-space plus a time dimension but 4D-space-time." It's relative. Clocks move faster or slower and distances expand or contract depending on the frame of reference of the measurer or viewer,

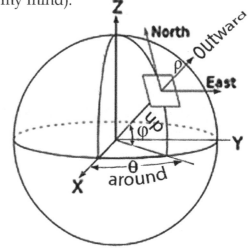

Carlo Rovelli has a section of his book <u>The Order of Time</u> called "The Dance of the Three Giants." Each of them had a theory of time and space:

• Aristotle said time measured the changing of things, no change no time and space was the relationships between things, no things no space.

• Newton believed in an ever-flowing time moving along independent of events and an ever-extending space independent of things. He saw time and space as the infinite stage upon which the mechanical workings of the world occurred. Newton's thought has permeated the way people think for over 300 years and the 3D Cartesian coordinate system was the way to express it along with an extra letter "t" that stood for time. An object is located at a point in space that can change in time.

• Einstein resolved the discrepancy between his two intellectual forefathers and their controversy over their relational and absolute theories of space, time, and motion. Einstein showed that gravity is time and space together and that time and space together are gravity. The gravitation field is informed by masses. The motions of masses are informed by gravity.

Rovelli reports that Gottfried Wilhelm Leibniz, a contemporary of Newton and co-inventor of the calculus, was prone to the ideas of Aristotle and disputed Newton on the absolute nature of time; so much so that he dropped the ubiquitous Newtonian "t" from his original last name "Leibnitz."

That Einstein was right and the others wrong, we know from the many tests of General Relativity over the last century. Gravity waves were detected in 2015. GPS systems and Google Maps must take into account the speeding up of time with the elevation of a clock and the slowing of time with increased relative speed. And all three are missing the spiritual dimension of which Rupert Spira says, "No Thought, No Time!" (see https://www.youtube.com/watch?v=8pMWF6-rSG0)

Three things the "power of Brahman" makes the mind do:
• Think
• Desire
• Will.

Carlo Rovelli has a section of his book <u>The Order of Time</u> called "The Dance of The Oscar Peterson Trio:
- Oscar Peterson on piano
- Ray Brown on bass
- Herb Ellis on guitar.

If you know about the 17th-century classical music of Bach, then check out the 20th-century classical music of Oscar Peterson! At concerts, he was introduced as "The Magnificent Oscar Peterson."

Vandana Shiva asserts that for humanity to have a future, creativity in the life sciences must include three levels:
- Creativity of living organisms that regenerate and evolve
- Creativity of indigenous communities whose knowledge systems conserve and utilize biodiversity
- Creativity of modern scientists respecting nature.

Arvind Kumar, a chest surgeon in Delhi for more than three decades said, "I don't see pink lungs even among healthy non-smoking young people... "The options for Delhi residents are three: (*See New York Times 11/8/2017*)
- To stop breathing. That is not possible.
- To quit Delhi. That is also not possible.
- To make the right to breathe fresh air a people's movement."

Charles Blow, writing in his New York Times column of 4/30/15, after the Baltimore riots and the death of Freddie Gray, said, "... America likes to hide its sins. This is because it wants its:

- Disaffected
- Dispossessed
- Disenfranchised

to use the door under the steps. This is because America sees its underclass as some sort of infinite sponge capable of quietly absorbing disadvantage, neglect, and oppression forever for the greater good of superficial calm and illusory order. And is expected to do so."

Walter Isaacson quotes Leonardo da Vinci giving a "Ted Talk" in the Sforza court of Milan in the late 15th century, "the painter has to depict:

- Light
- Shade
- Color

which the sculptor can generally ignore. Therefore, sculpture has fewer considerations and consequently requires less ingenuity." Leonardo also argued that painting should be considered one of the liberal arts on a par with poetry and not be classified as a mechanical art because, as we know today, "a picture is worth 1000 words;" assuming, of course, that the image has not been digitally manipulated (see Isaacson's book, Leonardo Da Vinci 2017)

The basic building blocks of life are:
- Water
- Organic compounds
- Energy.

Enceladus, a moon of the planet Saturn, has been shown to have all three. (Reported in the Economist of 8/8/2015)

At the railroad crossing, we must:
- Stop
- Look
- Listen.

The central dogma of molecular biology first enunciated by Francis Crick deals with the transfer of sequential information:

"DNA makes RNA makes protein."

The information does not flow backward from the protein. George Johnson, however, in *Scientific American 11/2014* questions the monoclonal theory of cancer development based on this dogma, suggesting that the development of cancer may be more complicated than we know.

Henry Giroux writes on "truthout.org" (4/11/2017) that cultures need enemies. In a society, governed by a ruthless notion of:
- Self-interest
- Privatization
- Commodification

more and more groups are demonized, cast aside and viewed as disposable. This includes poor Blacks, Latinos, Muslims, unauthorized immigrants, transgender communities and young people who protest the increasing authoritarianism of American society.

The alchemical:
- Sulfur …the spirit of life
- Salt… the base matter
- Mercury…the connector of the high and low

SULFER   SALT   MERCURY

"Mozart's Magic Flute", is a website by Phil Norfleet. He writes, "In my opinion, Wolfgang Amadeus Mozart's opera, 'The Magic Flute,' (Die Zauberflöte) is the greatest work of esoteric music ever written. The opera can be understood at three levels of meaning:
- Exoteric or popular level
- Mesoteric or Masonic level
- Esoteric or Rosicrucian level. "

Norfleet says that on the esoteric level, the opera is an alchemical allegory, an 18th century Enlightenment version of the ancient Egyptian Mysteries concerning the achievement of illumination. He deeply studies the opera from three vantage points. He says that on the stage, in *The Magic Flute*," there are three temples:
- Temple of Nature
- Temple of Reason
- Temple of Wisdom.

QUALITIES				
CARDINAL	♈ Aries	♑ Capricorn	♎ Libra	♋ Cancer
FIXED	♌ Leo	♉ Taurus	♒ Aquarius	♏ Scorpio
MUTABLE	♐ Sagittarius	♍ Virgo	♊ Gemini	♓ Pisces
	FIRE	EARTH	AIR	WATER	ELEMENT

The astrological:
- Cardinal
- Fixed
- Mutable.

Clare Martin wrote in <u>An Introduction to Psychological Astrology,</u> that the law of three can be observed in action in astrology. The three forces or modes are known as cardinal, fixed and mutable; or

- Initiating
- Resisting
- Mediating or accommodating.

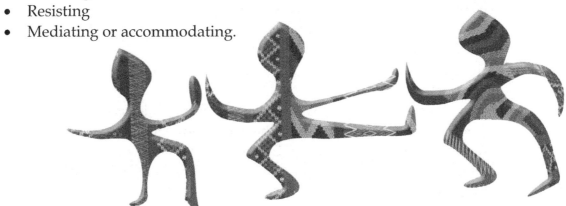

The three fundamental forces of nature:

- Activity *(passion, desire, energy, movement)*
- Inertia *(inertia, darkness, sloth, ignorance)*
- Balance *(truth, light, spirit, consciousness)*.

These are the three *Gunas* of Indian philosophy: *sattva, rajas, and tamas.*

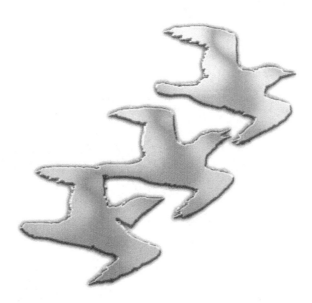

Robert Nozick, in his book, <u>The Examined Life,</u> wrote that Plato distinguished three parts of the soul:

- The rational part
- The courageous part
- The passions.

During the 2015 National Basketball Association playoffs, Baxter Holmes interviewed Dr. Chris Johnson for ESPN.com. Professionally, Dr. Johnson trains U.S. Special Operations Forces and was brought in to work with the champion Golden State Warriors basketball team. Both the basketball players and the soldiers must deal with stress and quick decision making, one with bullets flying and the other with a basketball moving around the court. Dr. Johnson cited three factors that, if present, will intensify stress:

- "If you perceive that a situation is something you've never done before, stress goes up.
- If you perceive the situation is uncontrollable, stress goes up.
- If you perceive the situation is unpredictable, stress goes up.

According to Dr. Johnson, "Everything we do whether it's here with the basketball team, or with special ops, is focused on changing those three perceptions."

The great front line of the Miles Davis quintet of the late nineteen fifties:
- Miles Davis on trumpet
- Cannonball Adderly on alto sax
- John Coltrane on tenor sax.

The Tri-Borough Bridge connects the three boroughs of Manhattan, the Bronx, and Queens. In lower Manhattan, three famous bridges cross over the East River to Brooklyn:

- The Williamsburg Bridge, (built 1903) from Houston Street on the lower east side of Manhattan to Williamsburg, Brooklyn neighborhoods where Hassidim, artists, yuppies, and Hispanics live.
- The Manhattan Bridge (built 1901) from Chinatown's Canal Street to downtown Brooklyn.
- The Brooklyn Bridge (built 1883) from the city hall area of Manhattan to Flatbush Avenue in downtown Brooklyn.

A world of:
- Things
- Substances
- Entities.

A triad from Carlo Rovelli's <u>The Order of Time</u>

A world of:
- Events
- Happenings
- Processes.

Another triad from Carlo Rovelli's <u>The Order of Time</u>

Three Worlds by Escher depict:
- Reflections of trees on the surface of the water
- Their fallen leaves on the surface
- Fish under the surface.

They were running, hiding, fighting, and running some more for a long time. Their journey was near its end. The three elementally weathered characters sat in the mouth of a scraggy cave panting hard to catch their breaths. They could hear the howling wolf pack in the forest below and the rumblings of the approaching army on the next mountain. The distant castle was finally in sight. Then one of them said, "All we have to do now is:
- Find the stone
- Get the girl
- Become kings."

A triad that is an illusion according to the Oneness schools:
- Knowledge
- Knower
- Knowing

Knowledge is not a thing that is acquired by another thing in the process of knowing something. There's no such thing as a thing!

The Three Stooges:
- Curly
- Mo
- Larry.

From the song, *"Hairstyles and Attitudes"*, lyrics by the rock group "Timbuk 3,"

"It may be just hype, but the latest findings cause me to tremble,
categorize us into three basic types. According to which of the
three stooges we most closely resemble."

Three forms of late twentieth-century pleasure:
- Sex
- Drugs
- Rock and roll

Jean Klein, the French Oneness teacher, discourses in his book, <u>I Am</u>, about how perception is the first message given by the senses before the brain starts naming. He invoked a Heisenberg-like principle where perception and concepts cannot exist simultaneously. He wrote, "He who is knowingly aware is simultaneously:

- Living witness
- Audience
- Actor

of the perceptions." He said that in everyday life we rarely give perceptions time to make themselves felt. We prematurely interfere with them by bringing forth memory-based concepts.

For it's

- One
- Two
- Three

strikes you're out at the old ball game.

The slogan of the Russian people during the revolution of 1917:

- Peace
- Bread
- Land

In his "Three Views of Marriage" article (NYT 2/23/16), David Brooks referred to the work of psychologist, Eli J. Finkel, who wrote that people now want marriage to satisfy their:

- Financial needs
- Emotional needs
- Spiritual needs.

Brooks wrote that there are, "three different but not mutually exclusive lenses" through which to think about marriage decisions:

- The psychological lens
- The romantic lens
- The moral lens.

"Looking through the first lens one seeks to avoid the neurotic, angry, or unstable person and wants to be attracted to an agreeable and nice person who has empathy. Through the second lens, one hopes the passion of romance will transform into a long-lasting love. Looking through the third lens can place marriage in the wider context of a society or philosophy."

The three harbingers of doom for the native peoples of the Americas:

- The Nina
- The Pinta
- The Santa Maria

In <u>Descartes Error</u>, Antonio Damasio wrote that an absence of emotions and feelings adversely effects our rationality --- a feature which makes us distinctly human and allows us to decide "in consonance with a sense of:

- A personal future
- Social convention
- Moral principle."

He gives examples of medical cases where patients with emotional defects having high IQs have great difficulty in making decisions affecting their personal lives such as deciding at which restaurant to dine, where to live, or which job take. Damasio devotes a chapter to the strange case of Phineas P. Gage who, while working on the railroad tamping explosive charges, had an accident in which a four-foot iron tamping rod blew off and up through his head to a height of 300 feet. He was walking around just after the accident. He died years later, in 1860, at the age of 37, but he was never quite the same as before the accident. Gage's skull and the tamping rod now reside in the Harvard University medical museum.

The destruction of the cultures of the native people of California, led by Father Junipero Serra and his followers, ensued because of:

- The church's missionary zeal
- The power of the Spanish military
- The ecological destruction by the Spanish settlers who brought with them:
    - Their illnesses which killed many people
    - Their herds of cattle and feed grains which destroyed many native species
    - Their greed and acquisitiveness for the land.

These facts were reported in the "San Francisco Chronicle" newspaper article by Lisbeth Haas (1/23/2015) because, what do you know, Pope Francis wants to make this guy Junipero a saint!

Meister Eckhart said, "The eye through which I see is the same eye through which God sees me. My eye and God's eye are a unity, he said,

- "One seeing
- One knowing
- One love."

The three drives that bind one if one is not established in Awareness of the Self:

- Desiring
- Doing
- Knowing.   *Vedanta Wisdom tradition*

Michael E. Webber discusses the great nexus of:

- Energy
- Water
- Food *(Scientific American 2/2015)*

When the constraints on the world's systems break, cascades of failures ensue. Examples abound:

- Pressure from population growth,
- Longer life spans
- Increased consumption.

In Frank Baum's political-economic symbolism in <u>The Wizard of Oz,</u> Dorothy is the American people and her three companions:

- The Tin Man is the industrial worker whose human body has been mechanized.
- The Scarecrow represents the Midwestern farmer being duped by the capitalists.
- The Cowardly Lion stands for Wm. Jennings Bryan, the great populist orator who despite his roar, had no real power.

Judy Garland starred in the 1939 Technicolor movie that lost to "Gone with The Wind" for best picture of the year. Later in the 20th century, Wikipedia reports, "The Wizard of Oz" became the most watched movie of all time.

Baum's spiritual symbolism in the <u>Wizard of Oz</u> --- Dorothy is the self who is trying to go home; the Wizard of Oz is a false ego and her three companions:

- The Tin Man is the body.
- The Scarecrow is the mind.
- The Cowardly Lion is the heart.

In the "Weapons of Mass Seduction: The Art of Propaganda" show at the DeYoung Museum in San Francisco (2018) a wall piece reads, "Today a single tweet can reach millions of people instantaneously. But prior to the internet age, spreading information and ideas to shape public opinion was more;

- Regulated
- Hierarchical
- Specialized."

In India, in 2012, 690 million people were blacked out when too many farmers blew the electric system by pumping groundwater during a drought. There is also stress in the Las Vegas water system:

- Power for Las Vegas casinos
- Water for the Hoover Dam to generate power for California
- Agricultural needs

"The Age of Protest," a column (NYT 1/13/16) in which Thomas Friedman wrote that protest is driven by the three largest forces on the planet:

- Globalization
- Moore's law
- Inequality

In his book, <u>Christ Actually</u>, James Carroll asks:
- How the texts about Jesus were originally written
- How they were interpreted early on
- How they can be understood in the contemporary world

To answer, he uses three different time frames:
- Lifetime of Jesus
- Era of 100 AD when the Roman empire was at war with the Israelites, destroyed their 1000-year-old temple, and when the gospels were written.
- "Present Secular Age, bracketed between the Nazi holocaust and the Hiroshima bomb - when faith in Jesus and the Gospels has become a problem unto itself." Carroll points out that if Jesus had died in the camps as a Jew or in Japan as a local resident, no religion would have sprung forth from his death.

Though "Big Bang" cosmology reduces life here on earth to insignificance; "Yet" Carroll said, "we are the puny creatures who:
- Know
- Think
- Love."

"The exquisite subtlety of human consciousness, " writes Carroll, "can account for everything but itself. Following, in effect, a three-stage movement:"
- Knowing
- Knowing that we know
- Knowing that we are known.

He sees consciousness leading to a primal consciousness that includes all consciousness in and of itself that leads to the God of religions.

The three guides:
- Tradition
- Experience
- Inspiration.

The three major TV networks that lost their market share going into the 21st century:
- ABC
- CBS
- NBC

Three lords of the 21st-century cloud:
- Amazon, which dominates US retail (4% of all retail in 2017)
- Google with 88% of online searches, and
- Facebook with a 77% share of the social media market in 2018.

Three techniques developed for magazine and radio advertising in the 1920s:
- "Demand Engineering" that creates consumer desires
- "Branding" which creates consumer loyalty
- "Targeted Advertising" which delivers the consciousness of specific consumers to the advertisers.

Using these methods, we see that Facebook has inadvertently "incubated a pervasive climate of rumor, propaganda, and conspiracy theories among its 2.2 billion user-customers" who are hooked to their screens and milked for their data. (see "They've Got You Where They Want You" by Jacob Weisberg ("New York Review of Books" 10/27/2016)

Arthur Schwartz and Howard Dietz wrote this verse in a famous song popularized by Frank Sinatra ...
- "You and
- the night and
- the music

fill me with flaming desire,
Setting my being completely on fire! ..."

The three coming technologies of the 21st century that can be used to produce weapons of mass destruction by organizations much smaller than the governments of nation-states:
- Genetics
- Robotics
- Nanotechnology
  see Bill Joy "Wired Magazine" April 2000

The San Francisco Chronicle News Services (2/20/16) reported that Chinese president, Xi Jimping, made a high-profile tour of three of his country's leading media outlets:

- "People's Daily," the Party newspaper
- Official Xinhua News Agency
- State broadcaster, China Central Television.

The leader told the editors and reporters that they must pledge absolute loyalty to the Communist Party and closely follow its leadership in:

- "Thought
- Politics
- Action."

In the United States, it's not so obvious but there is a <u>Manufacturing of Consent</u>, the famous book by Chomsky and Herman written in the analog age and updated for the digital age by Rob Williams on the "Project Censored" website of 2/16/2018.

The classic "big three" of the American automobile industry:

- General Motors
- Ford
- Chrysler

They ruled supreme in the years just after WWII, but since then have seemed to lose much of their market share. Maybe they just own all the stuff that's overseas.

Yuval Harari sees the evolution of economies as a progression from:

- Feudalism, to
- Capitalism to
- Dataism.

which is also a progression from:

- Management of land, to
- Management of machinery, to
- Management of data.

He points out that: controls over the ownership of land have evolved for 10,000 years; controls over the means of production have developed since the industrial revolution, but controls over the ownership of data have scarcely begun to evolve at all *(See Harari's YouTube talk given at the Davos Summit 2018)*

Richard Tarnas's triune prison of modern alienation is expressed in the ideas of:

- Copernicus
- Descartes
- Kant.

The ideas of these men led to the determinism of Newton and Laplace in which the world was viewed as analogous to the workings of a giant clock. Given the initial conditions of the positions and velocities of all the particles in the universe, the future was determined. Too bad that Leonardo's notebooks and his holistic worldview were lost for so long; (See Fritjof Capra, The Science of Leonardo) daVinci's work could have mitigated the development of such ideas as: "collateral damage", "human resources department", and the "ecological externalities" to economic growth. Tarnas sees the modern epidemic of alienation arising because we are not embedded in the environment but see ourselves as bagged-up selves whose consciousness is the only lit up thing there is, all else being stuff to be exploited for our needs, wants, amusement, and profits. Tarnas's book, The Passion of the Western Mind, is a history of western philosophy that reads like a novel.

In A Brief History of Thought, Luc Ferry has a different take than Richard Tarnas. He wrote that after Copernicus and Newton upset the apple cart, Descartes doubted everything, including social and religious authority, and even the existence of the chair upon which he sat. He doubted all certainties until he came to one...his own conscious subjectivity...."*Cogito Ergo Sum*...I think, therefore I am" Ferry said that the efforts of Descartes brought three new ideas to the history of thought:

- The centrality of subjectivity, the centrality of Man, and the responsibility of man.
- *Tabula rasa*, the idea that questions all authority and leads to revolution and to liberty, equality, and fraternity.
- Rejection of arguments from authority and from claims of absolute truth by the church or state.

Luc Ferry also said that Descartes added a new principle to the history of thought manifesting as a new theory of knowledge, a new ethics, and a new doctrine of salvation supplanting the ancient notion of the cosmos and the Christian God in Plato's *uber* world. Now "Man" was at the center and the Age of Humanism began.

In contrast to Luc Ferry, Antonio Damasio insists in <u>Descartes' Error</u> that the mind is embedded in the body. He bases his assertion on three statements:

- "The human brain and body constitute an indivisible whole.
- The organism interacts with the environment as an ensemble: interaction is neither of the body alone nor of the brain alone.
- The physiological operations that we call mind are derived from the structural and functional ensemble rather than from the brain alone."

Damasio writes that emotions and feeling point us in the right direction where, at some point, "we may put the instruments of logic to good use."

Three impossible things for the rational thinker, according to Indian spiritual leader, Mata Amritanandamayi:

- Love
- Surrender
- Faith

The sun of the three distresses that scorches the minds of spiritual seekers (according to Shankaracharya, Indian sage of the 8th century A.D.):

- The misery of body and mind.
- The misery of the perishability of creatures.
- The misery arising from the actions of the gods such as rain, wind, and lightning.

Search on the internet for "three ingredient meals." You will find:
- 3 cups of cherry tomatoes
- 15 ounce can of white beans
- 2 ounces of feta cheese.

Sauté the tomatoes in olive oil (3 minutes), add spice and beans for 10 (minutes), then add feta and serve.

The art of Dharma practice, wrote Stephen Batchelor in Buddhism Without Beliefs requires:
- Commitment
- Technical accomplishment
- Imagination

Luc Ferry gives three features of Kant's work about politics that opposes the aristocracy:
- Individualism
- Equality of status of people
- Value that is given to the idea of work.

Martin Scorsese's trilogy of New York movies:
- "Mean Streets"
- "Taxi Driver"
- "Raging Bull"

Mentioned by Paul Elie in NYT 11/21/2016

The most famous "spaghetti western" by director Sergio Leone is:
- The Good,
- The Bad, and
- The Ugly.

starring Clint Eastwood, Lee Van Cleef, and Eli Wallach. It's the third movie in his Dollars trilogy. "A Fistful of Dollars" and "For a Few Dollars More" are the first two movies in the series.

Three creative 20th century geniuses whose ideas extended our understanding out way beyond the confines of what Terence McKenna called "powdered wig rationality":
- Albert Einstein --- development of notions totally transforming our understanding of space, time, matter, and energy
- James Joyce --- bringing stream of consciousness to the novel and creatively redefining language in <u>Finnegan's Wake</u>
- John Coltrane --- spiritual and musical exploration into new worlds of expression. Eric Nissenson in his book <u>Ascension John Coltrane and His Quest</u> gives the similarities in the work of these three gentlemen.

Three rare things:
- Human birth
- Propensity to think about God
- Meeting with a God-realized sage.

This is what the wisdom teachers say.

Ozone, O₃, is a molecule made up of three oxygen atoms. In gaseous form, it has a pungent odor and is pale blue. It is unstable and toxic, being very harmful to life, especially as a lung irritant. In the atmosphere, however, it is very beneficial because it absorbs damaging ultraviolet radiation and prevents it from reaching life here on the earth's surface...See Wikipedia.

Peggy D. Snyder's <u>10 Minute Cognitive Workout</u> begins with a discussion of cognitive restructuring that eliminates thoughts which are:
- Negative
- Irrational
- Dysfunctional.

and replaces them with thoughts that are:
- Positive
- Rational
- Functional.

A popular song encourages us to "accentuate the positive
- Eliminate the negative
- Latch on to the affirmative, and
- Don't mess with Mister In-Between."   by Harold Arlen and Johnny Mercer

Viktor Frankl's three possible ways to find meaning in life:

- A deed we do, a work we create
- An experience, a human encounter, a love
- When confronted with unchangeable fate (such as an incurable disease), a change of attitude toward fate.

His major work is <u>Man's Search for Meaning</u>.

The Three Musketeers:

- Athos
- Porthos
- Aramis

and their friend D'Artagnan had this slogan: "All for One and One for All."
Check out ..."Lust, Love, and Loyalty: The Three Musketeers".... @
https://genxmedia.wordpress.com/2014/02/07/lust-love-and-loyalty-the-three-musketeers/

Meister Eckhart's three points about the poor in spirit who inherit the kingdom of heaven:

- A poor man is one who wants nothing and desires nothing.
- A poor man is one who knows nothing.
- A poor man is one who has nothing.

The slogan of the early twentieth-century Indian reformer Sri Narayan Guru:

- One caste
- One God
- One religion

Beethoven's "Trio in A flat minor for violin, cello, and piano."

The three powers of the Goddess:

- Her will
- Her Knowledge
- The Action She takes to create this universe out of her very own Being.

The three monkeys who respectfully:
- Hear no evil
- See no evil
- Speak no evil.

Wikipedia says that in Japanese these monkeys are called *Mizaru, Kikazaru,* and *Iwazaru* and that the understanding of them originally came to Japan with a Tendai-Buddhist legend from 8th century China. Their images appear in various shrines throughout Japan.

Cathy O'Neil uses the term WMD's, in her book, <u>Weapons of Math Destruction</u> to denote mathematical models or algorithms that claim to quantify important traits: teacher quality, recidivism risk, and credit-worthiness, but have harmful outcomes and often reinforce inequality, keeping the poor poor and the rich rich. Reviewing the book for "Scientific American," Evelyn Lamb (8/2016) said that WMD's have three things in common:
- Opacity
- Scale
- Damage.

They are often proprietary or otherwise shielded from prying eyes, so they have the effect of being a black box. Lamb quotes O'Neil, "in Florida, adults with clean driving records and poor credit scores paid an average of $1552 more for insurance than the drivers with excellent credit and a drunk driving conviction."

The three aspects of the bird of spiritual practice:
- Wing of doing work on one's self
- Wing of doing selfless service
- Guiding tail feather of knowledge.

The rhythm section of the classical Count Basie big band:
- Jo Jones on drums
- Walter Page on bass
- Freddy Green on rhythm guitar

..."get up in the morning and look at the world in a way that takes nothing for granted.
- Everything is phenomenal
- Everything is incredible
- Never treat life casually.

To be spiritual is to be amazed." — Abraham Joshua Heschel

Three worlds in which we might live:
- Mundane world
- Supernatural world
- Shamanistic bridge between them.

Epicawesomewolf @ Wikimedia Commons

There is revolution in the in the air of our current networked world writes Joshua Cooper Ramo in his book, <u>The Seventh Sense</u>. Could the simple act of this worldwide connection, he asks, "change how we think about all historical questions, the ones that decide if we live in an era of peace or one of:
- Fear
- Uncertainty
- Tragedy?"

Federal laws bar employers from firing workers because of these labels:
- Race
- Religion
- Gender.

A trio of masterful 21st-century virtuosos:
- Béla Fleck---banjo
- Zakir Hussain---tabla
- Edgar Meyer--- bass

who move with ease among quite a few of the world's musical traditions.

Society has been organized over the years by:
- employers and employees
- lords and serfs
- masters and slaves

Richard Wolff points out that the employees produce the wealth that the employers get into their hands thereby getting wealthier and excluding the working people from sharing the surplus wealth they have created.

The threefold dignity of modernity according to Ken Wilber:
- Equality
- Freedom
- Justice.

The three maidens in "The Pilgrim's Progress":
- Faith
- Hope
- Charity

"Stop Googling. Let's Talk" (NYT 9/27/15), Sherry Turkle's piece is about the lack of empathy amongst the "app" generation. "To reclaim conversation for yourself, your friendships and society," she wrote, "push back against viewing the world as one giant app. It works the other way, too: Conversation is the antidote to the algorithmic way of looking at life because it teaches you about:
- Fluidity
- Contingency
- Personality."

The three miseries as stated by the ancient Indian sage, Ashtavakra:
- The organism
- Other organisms
- Nature.

The three difficulties in the *lojong dharma* training taught by Pema Chodron:

- Seeing our neurosis as neurosis
- Breaking out of habitual patterns by doing something different,
- Continuing on the way of living in a state of being awake even when your life seems to be unraveling.

Listening to the radio as I ride in a car, three sounds I cognize immediately are:

- The fundamentalist preacher before he utters a "thee" or a "thou"
- The dulcet tones of the NPR lady informing you about the wonders of her sponsor
- The self-righteous tones of pundits (left or right) pridefully intoning their private special secret knowledge that exposes the "real truth." They sound almost but not quite like the fundamentalist preacher' evincing an ego bound more to the words of newspapers than to the words of scriptures.

A search on Google for "the three L's" turns up the three L's" of Christine Lagarde for women's empowerment:

- Learning
- Labor
- Leadership.

and a visit to the dentist shows a poster on the wall saying:

- Live   life passionately
- Laugh   until your belly hurts
- Love   unconditionally

with the hope that the pain killer holds below the sounds of drilling.

The three major problems of the twenty-first century:
- nuclear war
- climate change
- technological disruption

will require a global effort for their solutions. This is the takeaway from Yuval Harari's Penguin Publishers 2018 annual lecture in India. He said that while the job of nationalism is to protect the citizens of a nation, one nation cannot build a wall to stop nuclear war, stop the proliferation of nefarious deeds on the internet, or abate global warming

David Brooks (NYT 2/20/15) wrote that religious extremism exists on three levels:
- The way it grows out of economic and political dysfunction
- The way it is generated by perverted spiritual zeal
- The way it is organized by religious beliefs.

What you want from your financial advisor is that he or she has the:
- Time
- Energy
- Expertise

to participate in the financial marketplace.

Three broad categories of progressive expenditure are:
- investment
- benefits enhancement
- major system overhaul

which can fiscally be paid for by taxes on the rich, taxes on everyone for enhanced services like Medicare for all, and loans for infrastructure that will pay dividends in better lives for the citizens.   (Paul Krugman NYT 2/20/2019)

Video Games: The Secret Life" ("*New York Review of Books*" 10/8/2015) by Gabriel Winslow-Yost reviews books on video games. In looking at the book, Gamelife: a Memoir, by Michael W. Clune, Winslow-Yost asked how could a game matter so much since the player of a game exists in a world that contains, quoting Clune, " three feelings:
- Victory
- Defeat
- Frustration."

Noam Chomsky's three thieves of modern peoples' power and dignity:

- Fascism
- Bolshevism
- Capitalistic corporate tyranny.

Harari seems to be more upbeat than Chomsky when he writes that there were three main twentieth century stories:

- fascism
- communism
- liberalism.

With the demise of the first two, the only story left was global liberalism in which "walls, moats, and barbed wire were replaced by open roads, wide bridges, and bustling airports." This was the "global mantra" in the 1990s and 2000s. But after the financial meltdown of 2008 and by 2016, the story is being retold. The "civilized world" now sees itself floating on only a thin crust of stability. See Harari's book 21 Lessons for the 21st Century

And Chomsky has a heart. He said that Social Security is based on the principle that you care about other people. You care, for example, whether the disabled widow across town is going to get enough to eat. The ideas behind this principle:

- Solidarity
- Sympathy
- Mutual support

are doctrinally dangerous to the power elite. They do not want a social safety net. Their preferred doctrine is just, "care for yourself, don't care about anyone else." The ideas that:

- We are all in it together
- We care about each other
- We have responsibility for one another

are frightening to the rulers who want a society which is dominated by:

- Power
- Authority
- Wealth

a society in which people are passive and obedient.
See https://www.youtube.com/watch?v=RfKSSnYxAnk

The US economy grew from the end of WWII throughout the rest of the 20th century, but workers' wages stagnated starting in the late 1970s. People coped with this in three ways to keep up their standard of living:

• women left the household to go to work
• people worked harder and longer
• people used the rising value of their homes as collateral for loans

With the subprime real estate collapse of 2007-08, the people's anger arose to be voiced in the Tea Party and Occupy movements, each sharing a similar rhetoric according to Robert Reich in a talk given in Berkeley in February 2019

Pope Francis addressed the Second World Meeting of Popular Movements, a congress of global activists working to mobilize and help the poor in Bolivia during the summer of 2015. The New York Times reported that many people wore Che Guevara T-shirts while some indigenous women wore traditional black bowlers. Pope Francis said, "I would even say that the future of humanity is in great measure in your own hands, through your ability to organize and carry out creative alternatives, through your daily efforts to ensure the three L's:

• Labor
• Lodging
• Land."

Illiberal populists all over the world were benefiting from three simultaneous backlashes to progress in the early 21st century, writes John Feffer (commondreams.org 8/27/2016):

- Cultural backlash against civil rights, multiculturalism, women's rights, and gay rights
- Economic backlash against globalization and the wealth gap
- Political backlash against democratic governments caught in the chaos of partisanship (Some warts on the head of this monster are: Bolsonaro, Duterte, La Penn, Modi, Netanyahu, Orbán, Putin, and Trump.

Stephen Bachelor's three things that need tending, like a garden:

- Ethical integrity
- Focused awareness
- Understanding.

Karen Armstrong was being interviewed by Mitch Jezerich on radio KPFA about her book, <u>Fields of Blood</u>. She referred to Lord Acton, who late in the nineteenth century, warned of an Achilles' heel of the nation-state --- the stress it put on:

- Ethnicity
- Culture
- Language

because people who did not fit the national profile were vulnerable to enslavement or extermination. It's obvious that history bears him out again and again and again, even though there might not be Red States or Blue States but just the United States.

A BBC nature film on the jungles shows a troop of chimpanzees moving single file through the undergrowth to attack a neighboring troop, steal their fruits, and commit cannibalism. We are not much better in the age of ISIS or in the Dutch enlightened period (1660s), when Descartes and Spinoza lived in the progressive milieu of Amsterdam, and when a mob attacked the liberal mayor. On the way to bring him to the gallows, they flayed his body, quartered it, and hung the pieces to rot in the public square. (see Antonio Damasio <u>Looking for Spinoza</u>) More recently in 2013, Buddhist monks have been involved in depredations of the Muslim Rohingyas in western Burma. Some Buddhist monks were also involved in the final battle of the Hindu-Buddhist war at the Ninthi Kadal lagoon (2009) in Sri Lanka (See Joshua Hammer New York Review of Books 3/5/15). The UN Human Rights Council is investigating the atrocities in deaths of over 40,000 civilians and fighters. What's needed:

- Truth
- Justice
- Accountability.

Remember the Turkish genocide of Armenians (1919), the shooting and lynching of 4 black people in Walton County Georgia (1946), or the lynching's of Mexicans in the American southwest during the 19th and 20th centuries. And now we ape the chimps in a sanitary digital dronish way.

<u>Killing the Host: How Financial Parasites and Debt Bondage Destroy the Global Economy</u> author Michael Hudson spoke with Amy Goodman on the "Democracy Now" radio program during the financial jitters of August 2015. He said Wall Street is running things. It is Casino Capitalism. They are not investment banks but betting parlors. It is the Fire Sector of:

- Finance
- Insurance
- Real estate

that are the parasites feeding and weakening

- Labor
- Government
- Industry itself

They are using their profits, of late, to buy back stock in order to increase stock prices and benefit the 1% class instead of investing in endeavors fruitful to the future of society.

Three fictions of market capitalism
- Labor is a commodity. People are resources. This inspired the works of Marx. People allow themselves to be commoditized because they fall for the myth that having stuff is more important than being.
- Land is a commodity. The land is nature. This is at the heart of the present ecological crisis.
- Money is a commodity over and above being a medium of exchange, which leads to the present situation that there exist hundreds of trillions of dollars of marketable financial instruments, "worth" much more than the global economy is "worth" ...from a talk by Thomas Powers, broadcast on radio station KPFA in early 2015.

19TH AND 20TH-CENTURY OWNERS, WORKERS, AND FACTORIES

"On the "Relationship Economy" website (http://www.relationship-economy.com), Dan Robles contributed an article, "Factors of Production for An Innovation Economy." He wrote that these factors were land, capital, and labor one hundred years ago but now the factors in the Innovation Economy are:
- Intellectual Capital (also called Human Capital)
- Social Capital using contacts and social media
- Creative Capital - "engineers and scientists think more like artists and musicians than like production workers"

"Adbusters," the magazine that spurred on the Occupy Movement of 2011, had this bit in their 9/2016 issue: "the three most fascist industries that we must reinvent:
- Finance
- Fashion
- Food."

Paul Krugman wrote, "Wealth can be bad for your soul" in his New Year's Day 2016 article (NYT) titled:

- Privilege
- Pathology
- Power.

He said that this is not just an old wives' tale but is supported by recent research and cited an article by Maia Szalavitz who reported that:

"Wealthier people are more likely to cut people off in traffic and to behave unethically in simulated business and charity scenarios." Earlier that year, statistics on charitable giving revealed that while the wealthy donate about 1.3% of their income to charity, the poorest actually give more than twice as much as a proportion of their earnings — 3.2%." (http://healthland.time.com/2013/08/20/wealthy-selfies-how-being-rich-increases-narcissism/)

In the Showtime TV series, "The Untold History of the United States", historian Peter Kuznick and movie-maker Oliver Stone elucidated three myths:

- America won WWII
- Russia started the Cold War
- Hiroshima and Nagasaki bombs were needed to force Japan to surrender.

The Russians lost 25 million people in defeating 25 crack German divisions while the Americans lost 400,000 soldiers confronting only 3 or 4 German Divisions on the western front. On the third point, the Japanese wanted to surrender to the Americans rather than face a Russian invasion from the north. On the second point...*I dunno*. Was Russia just a 3rd world country facing the world empire that needed a boogie man to feed its military-industrial complex?

The 3 G's of the Spanish Conquest of the New World:
- Gold
- Glory
- God.

This trio of motivating factors along with superior technology and disease would prove to be the fuel that propelled the Spanish conquest of the New World. The legacy of Spanish culture and the tragedy of the extermination of the indigenous peoples of these areas would change the course of the world forever. See the blog: http ://project-history.blogspot.com/2005/10/spanish-motivations-in-new-world-gold.html

Escher's drawing Moebius Strip1, which, he said, looks like three fish, each eating the tail of another
easier to see in color

The shadow side in the development of the American Empire:
- Genocide of native people
- African slavery
- Greed

On its website of 3/17/15, the "Daily Kos" headlines its article by Doctor Jazz with "Religion, Racism & the Consequences of the Republican Policy:

- Poverty
- Obesity
- Incarceration.

Texas was settled by frontiersmen and frontierswomen who brought with them:

- A rifle
- An ax
- A Bible.

Written by Thomas Powers in his article, "Texas: the Southern Baptists in Power"
"New York Review of Books" 10/9/2014

Powers also said that Ronald Reagan and his advisors sensed that Texas Baptists were at the heart of a major change in America; a counterrevolution to modernity and the three most disturbing things to these fundamentalists were:

- End of slavery
- Theory of evolution
- Emancipation of women

Yuval Harari wrote in a section of <u>Sapiens</u>, called "American Purity," that the American choice to import slaves from Africa was due to 3 factors:

- Africa was closer than say Vietnam
- The slave trade was already well established in Africa by the Muslim traders
- Africans had more immunity to malaria and other tropical diseases of the deep south than northern people like the Irish who could have been indentured.

In the early days of the 1600s, the hardcore nature of slavery had not, yet, set in, but soon the main myths were developed to justify white supremacy. Harari wrote that:

- Theologians said Africans were descended from the sons of Ham, son of Noah, and were cursed in the scripture to endure slavery.
- Biologists said the Africans did not have a mentality as developed as the whites.
- Sociologists said the Africans were dirty, slothful, and disease-ridden.

I've heard, that upon the first contact, people of the Eastern lands thought the Europeans stunk to high heavens, probably because they bathed so seldom.

Arlie Russell Hochschild's book <u>Strangers in a Strange Land: Anger and Mourning on the American Right,</u> is reviewed by Nathaniel Rich in the "New York Review of Books" *(11/10/16)*. Hochschild tried to overcome the "empathy wall" that separates left from right in the hope of coming to an understanding of the other side. Also, to see through their eyes and to understand the links between:

- Life
- Feeling
- Politics

Ken Wilber's three factors for the skillful practice of abiding in oneness:
- Active attention
- Stopping of thought, concepts, objectification, and mental chatter
- Unity of sight, seer, and seen

Averroës, the medieval Arab philosopher, distinguished three levels of reason:
(From Arthur Herman, <u>The Cave and the Light</u>")
- The ordinary person whose mind is satisfied with parables and injunctions from scriptures
- The educated person who wants something more than the word of God but who is content when faith wins out over reason
- The person of reason who is imbued with Aristotelian logic and the science of substance and potentiality.

Aristotle's three causes for the creation of anything:

- Material cause
- Instrumental cause
- Efficient cause.

E.g., in the creation of a pot: there is the clay, the potter's wheel, and the potter. In the creation of chaos, there is the disaffected populous, the demagogue, and the news of the day.

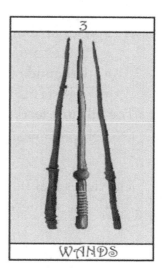

Aristotle's three forms of knowledge:

- *Episteme:* knowing and understanding
- *Praxis*: practicality, as in politics and ethics
- *Techne:* making things, i.e. blacksmithing.

Thomas Friedman quotes Dov Seidman who said that the world can be divided into three kinds of regions: *(NYT 8/23/2014)*

- Countries of "sustainable order" or order based on shared values, stable institutions, and consensual politics,
- Countries with "imposed order" or order based on an iron-fisted, top-down leadership, or propped-up by oil money, or combinations of both, but no real shared values or institutions, and
- Whole regions of disorder, such as Iraq, Syria, Central America and growing swaths of Central and North Africa, where there is neither an iron fist from above nor shared values from below to hold states together anymore.

A triple-double in basketball occurs when a player
- Scores more than 10 points
- Rebounds the ball more than 10 times
- Assists his teammates in making their shots more than 10 times

The all-time leaders for this achievement in the National Basketball Association are Lebron James, Jason Kidd, Russell Westbrook, and Magic Johnson."

The riches that flowed from slave ownership was threefold:
- the value of the slaves themselves, both as capital and as security for loans;
- the value of the product they produced, including more slaves; and
- the value of the land they cleared and planted.
  See <u>Slave Nation: How Slavery United the Colonies and Sparked The American Revolution</u> by Alfred and Ruth Blumrosen

In Spanish-speaking countries, the three stars of Orion's Belt are called Las Tres Marías, three Marys or Maries who were present at the resurrection of Jesus:
- Mary, mother of Jesus
- Mary Magdalene
- Mary of Clopas (John 19:25)

In her book, <u>Biopiracy - The Plunder of Nature and Knowledge,</u> Vandana Shiva explains the three waves of globalization:
- 1st wave: colonization of non-European areas of the world (500 years
- 2nd wave: imposition of the Western idea of "development" during the post-colonial period since WWII
- 3rd wave: era of "free trade", a re-colonialization on the micro scale of genetic modification and the patenting of indigenous ideas and materials. The developed world is spreading monoculture fortified by intellectual property rights.

Capabilities made possible by continued practice and effort-- the abilities to ride:

- Tricycles
- Bicycles
- Unicycles

Cornel West was interviewed in the "New York Times", 8/20/15. The interviewer, George Yancy, asked, "When it comes to race in America in 2015, what is to be done?" Brother West said, " You've got to shatter:

- Denial
- Avoidance
- Evasion."

The three that is a crowd

Some romantic triads:

- Two men vying for the same woman
- A woman torn between her desires for two men
- A man torn between his desires for two women
- A ménage à trois
- Two people vying for a third person
- A relationship based upon
  - A flirtation
  - An affair
  - A long term marriage

https://www.thisiswhyimbroke.com/reindeer-menage-a-trois-sweater/

David Brooks *(NYT 7/11/14)* said, "Most of us spend our days thinking we are playing baseball, but we are really playing soccer. We think we individually choose what career path to take, whom to socialize with, what views to hold. But, in fact, those decisions are shaped by the networks of people around us more than we dare recognize. "This influence can happen in these three ways:

- "Contagion -- People absorb memes, ideas, and behaviors from each other like the way they catch a cold
- Structure of your network -- People behave differently depending on the structure of their social network
- Structure of an industry-- The time and culture of an industry influence innovation (e.g. computers now, Broadway shows in earlier decades)."

Amritanandamayi's three important qualities needed in a spiritual pursuit:

- Patience
- Optimistic faith
- Enthusiasm.

Three fundamentals postulated by all religions:

- World
- Soul
- God

which, according to Ramana Maharshi, stay as three only so long as the ego lasts. He was born in 1896. At age 17, Ramana went through a transformation in consciousness. He felt as if he had died and awoke to a new state, perceiving himself as an essence independent of the body. During this process, he felt himself to be an eternal entity, existing without reliance on the physical body or material world. He soon left his home and made his way to the temple in the town of Tiruvanamalai at the foot of the holy mountain, Arunachala, in South India, where pilgrimage continues since long ago. Ramana first lived inside the temple, then in Virupaksha cave up on the mountain above the temple, and finally down the mountain at his ashram. His sparse oeuvre of writings came about only at the request of his devotees. Ramana sat on his couch surrounded by devotees in a small meditation hall for hours at a time. He taught in silence. He had time to himself when he took his daily walk on his beloved mountain. (See the ashram's website www.arunachala.org/ramana/life, his collected writings, and the wonderful discourses of archivist David Godman on YouTube.)

On the brainyquote.com website, this gem by Hannah Arendt can be found. "This is the precept by which I have lived:
- Prepare for the worst,
- expect the best, and
- take what comes."

The Coca-Cola Corporation has spent billions of dollars over the years advertising an attractive intimate connection of its product to:
- youth
- health
- sports

and billions of people are affected subconsciously; they do not think about Coke's link to obesity and diabetes. This tidbit is taken from Harari's chapter "Post-Truth" in <u>his 21 Lessons for the 21st Century</u>.

The Remusian Triad as sung by Uncle Remus in the song "Zippity Do Dah" which refers to the bluebird that was sitting on his shoulder as he did his St. Francis routine walking down a country road singing...

"Zippity Do Dah. Zippity A.

Mr. Bluebird's on my shoulder
- It's the Truth
- It's Actual
- Everything is Satisfactual".

"Zippity Do. Dah Zippity A. My Oh My what a wonderful day!

(see the movie that's no longer PC, "Song of the South." Uncle Remus was a slave. James Baskett won an Oscar in 1948 for his role, but he could not attend the grand opening of the movie held in segregated Atlanta, Ga.)

Patanjali's threefold foundation for yogic attainment:
- Concentration of the mind on one point
- Continuance of that concentration in meditation
- *Samadhi*, a state of merging into the concentration and into the point.

He compiled a book of aphorisms, The Yoga Sutras, around 2000 years ago. The first three aphorisms are:
- "Yoga is the restraint of mental modifications"
- "Then the seer dwells in his own nature,"
- "Otherwise he is of the same form as the modifications."

Ramdev, an entrepreneurial snake oil salesman and yogi, is influential in Indian BJP right-wing politics (2018). He's made billions from the products produced by his Patanjali Corp, a leader in the FMCG (fast moving consumer goods) market. This is reported in the Sunday Times Magazine (7/22/2018) by Robert F. Worth. Patanjali won't be turning over in his grave because he was never buried, and he was a realized master who wouldn't give a damn.

The three bestselling items of yoga merchandise in the American market are:
- Yoga spandex tights
- Yoga mats
- Yoga blocks and bolsters

In the summer of 2013, a great scandal developed when it was disclosed that tight-fitting women's yoga pants in the Foocelon brand were see-through. The scandal got hot when the CEO of the company claimed that it was the fault of women's bodies, not his product. Stephen Colbert reported that in the months before the scandal broke, enrollment of men in yoga classes had increased considerably.

Three types of motivational systems of the neuroscientists:
- Seeking system
- Threat system
- Caring system

The first is concerned with wanting, pursuing, achieving, consuming with drive, excitement, and impatience. The second is concerned with safety seeking and protection and displays anxiety, anger, and disgust. The last one is concerned with caring and soothing, and with connectedness, love, safety, and contentment. See Caring Economics: Conversations on Altruism and Compassion between Scientists, Economists, and the Dalai Lama edited by Tania Singer and Matthieu Ricard.

Divas of the Motown sound, the Supremes:
- Diana Ross
- Mary Wilson
- Florence Ballard

Wikipedia reports that the Supremes were the premier act of Motown Records during the 1960s. They were one of the most popular singing groups of all time, even rivaling the Beatles. 12 of their single records are found on Billboard's top 100 of all time including "Stop! In the Name of Love", "You Keep Me Hanging On", and "Someday We'll Be Together". Martha and the Vandellas was another great Motown girl group, also inducted into the Rock and Roll Hall of Fame with hits such as "Dancing in the Street", "Heat Wave", and "Nowhere to Run." Their original members were Rosaland Ashford, Martha Reeves, and Betty Kelley. Gladys Knight & the Pips was another great group with Gladys singing with three guys. Their great hit record was "I Heard It Through the Grapevine."

Three ingredients of a good scandal that has legs for more than a few of the media's news cycles:
- A highly elected official
- Who is a religious fundamentalist
- Having a juicy, adulterous affair.

Clinton wasn't a fundamentalist, but he did conjure some creative metaphysics on the nature of the word "is." Of the 22 people on Wikipedia's entry List of federal political sex scandals in the United States Congress for 2010-2018 seventeen were Republicans and five were Democrats. While adultery was most common, homosexuality, harassment, child pornography, and penis exposure on the internet were also alleged.

The three branches of our government under the One God We Trust.
- Executive
- Legislative
- Judicial.

Ta-Nehisi Coates gives the big three that "bonded white people in a broad aristocracy united by the salient fact of their unblackness":
- Slavery
- Jim Crow
- Segregation   (from his book, <u>We Were Eight Years in Power</u>)

John A. Powell states that 3 fears pervade American society:
- Fear of war,
- Economic fear
- Racial fear

He wrote that these fears are fostered by a society constructed on 3 levels: the elites, the whites, and the blacks. In his book, <u>Racing to Justice</u>, he noted that elite John Smith married the elite Pocahontas, but in the South, there were the miscegenation laws that were later to inspire the Nazis. Also, the non-elite whites are tasked by the elites to police the blacks. This system is perpetuated by a three-party political system:
- Democrats
- Republicans
- The South

It might be argued, however, that the last two items on the list have merged into the Red State areas by the turn of the 21st-century. In the early 20th century, the Democratic Party was dominated by the Dixiecrats who made deals with the elites in return for support for Jim Crow. The South was outraged by the New Deal social welfare and back to work programs that did not respect racial difference. With the civil rights movement, the South realigned with the Republicans who gave support for their racial program in return for support for the elite hegemony.

Haider Javed Warraich ("What Our Cells Teach Us About a 'Natural' Death," in The Stone section of the "New York Times" (3/13/2017) states that cells die via three main mechanisms:

- Necrosis, "The ugliest and least elegant form of cell death ... in which, because of either a lack of food or some other toxic injury, cells burst open, releasing their contents into the serum",
- Autophagy, " in which the cell turns on itself, changing its defective or redundant components into nutrients, which can be used by other cells. This form of cell death occurs when food supply is limited", and
- Apoptosis, "a programmed form of cell death. When a cell becomes old or disrepair sets in, it is nudged, usually by signaling molecules, to undergo a form of controlled self-demolition."

Hydras are minute long tubular organisms with a ring of tentacles around their mouths. Their simple neural networks oversee the entire gastronomical process:

- ingestion
- digestion
- excretion.

See The Strange Order of Things "Life, Feeling, and the Making of Cultures." by Antonio Damasio

The three types of persons involved in the higher levels of the military-industrial complex:

- Politicians and bureaucrats
- Military personnel
- Corporate executives.

All the same people changing their costumes and makeup from time to time.

Three of the most "blankety-blanks" in the history of the U.S.A, until 2016:

- Bush
- Cheney
- Rumsfeld

Three sources for the mainstream media's news:

- Potus*   *President of the United States susceptible to the Dark Triad: narcissism, Machiavellianism, and psychopathy*
- Flotus*   *First Lady of the United States*
- Scotus*   *Supreme Court of the United States*

Three rascals in Soviet Russia's history:

- Marx
- Lenin
- Stalin

But here, ol' Karl is taking a bad rap. He provided prescient criticism and he didn't kill anybody.

Antony Beevor reviews the book, <u>Blitzed: Drugs in the Third Reich</u> by Norman Ohler. The Nazi ideology demanded purity of:
- Body
- Blood
- Mind   *(New York Review of Books 03/09/2017)*

Thus, junkies were to be exterminated, but Hitler was a junky himself, being injected regularly with cocktails that included glucose, cocaine, morphine, and pig's liver by his decorated doctor, Theodor Morell. The whole country was strung-out on a kind of meth marketed as Pervitin. It was certainly given to the soldiers performing their blitzkriegs for days on end without sleep. Drug makers Merck and Bayer were involved. The students were popping bennies big time. Pervatin was the drug of choice for nurses working the night shift, stressed out businessmen, and women trying to live up to their duties of:
- Kinder   ...children
- Kuche   ...cooking
- Kirche   ...church

as encouraged by Nazi dogma.

In his book, *On Tyranny*, Timothy Snyder writes that the Nazi SS expanded their "lawless zones" in the concentration camps to all of occupied Europe. The SS
- Began as an organization outside the law
- Became an organization that transcended law, and
- Ended up an organization that undid law.

Steve Bannon said of the 2016 election, "We got elected on
- 'Drain the swamp'
- 'Lock her up'
- 'Build the wall'

...anger and fear are what gets people to the polls."

Mantra of the Republicans:
- Power
- Wealth
- Fame

Mantra of people showing compassion:
- May all the people
- In all worlds
- Be happy.

Mantra of the Democrats:
- Fame
- Wealth
- Power

One of the *mahavakyas,* the great sayings of the Vedas:
- Thou
- Art
- That

The dualistic saying of Descartes (I think therefore I am):
- *Cogito*
- *Ergo*
- *Sum*   *(see A Short History of Thought by Luc Ferry)*

A knowing implying being as if they are two separate things, yet establishing a subjectivity that is the same for both the royalty and commoners alike thus influencing the French Revolution and the eventual rise of liberal democracies.

Ram Das, the American spiritual teacher, brought a great mantra to the modern world that is very different from the previously mentioned dictum of Descartes':

- Be
- Here
- Now

I had always thought that the source of the following mantra was a 1940s movie by the comedians, Abbot and Costello, but I was shocked when my research on the internet led me to the, far from politically correct, bit in a Popeye cartoon. Popeye is sitting on a throne, ensconced in his slick colonial ego, surrounded by a circle of dark-skinned people wearing grass skirts bowing up and down and intoning:

- Salami
- Salami
- Baloney (search for this mantra on youtube.com then check below https://groups.google.com/forum/#!msg/rec.arts.tv/l2vtsCDjEvI/fQfWdprZWdlJ)

This reminds me of the white supremacists surrounding Trump intoning "Send Her Back, Send Her Back, Send Her Back." Trump's mother didn't emigrate from Scotland until 1930 and his wife, "the model," came in the 1990's. Back to Popeye, in their language, the people were telling Popeye, "Go home white mother feather."

The comedy rule of three, said Andy Kindler, is based on:

- Setup
- Second example to set up the pattern
- Kicker that breaks the expected pattern

John Kinde (http://www.humorpower.com/art-rulethree.html) uses the rule on his telephone answering machine: "Sorry I can't personally answer the phone.

- I'm either motivating thousands of people,
- Appearing on the Oprah show, or
- Taking a nap.

Please leave a message and I'll return your call when I wake up."

The three R's:

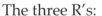

- readin'
- 'ritin'
- 'rithmatic

Three causes for the levels of the planet's seas to be rising are given in John Gertner's article, "The Secrets in Greenland's Ice Cap Sheet." (*"New York Times 11/12/2015*)

- At warmer temperatures, water expands and thus the oceans get bigger.
- The world's mountain glaciers are rapidly melting and draining into the seas.
- The polar ice sheets are shedding meltwater and icebergs at an accelerating rate.

Gertner reports that Greenland is now experiencing an average net loss of about 303 billion tons of ice every year and that such losses, according to the scientific consensus, will lead to a rise of the sea level by a foot or so by the end of the 21st century.

Humans ... are meaning-seeking animals, wrote David Brooks in his NYT column (11/17/2015) just after the horrendous Paris terrorist attacks. He quotes Rabbi Jonathan Sacks who said that we live in a century that "has left us with a maximum of choice and a minimum of meaning." The secular substitutes for religion:

- Nationalism
- Racism
- Political ideology

have all led to disaster. So many people flock to religion, sometimes — especially within Islam (but not exclusively)— to extremist forms of pathological expression.

In this age of terror, we struggle to figure out how to protect ourselves —
especially in 2015, from "active shooters". The Federal Bureau of Investigation
and the Department of Homeland Security have promoted a suggestion to help
us figure out how to protect ourselves from these "active shooters." Their dictum
is

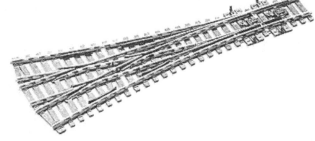

- Run
- Hide
- Fight

In his "Gray Matter" article, Joseph Ledoux, (*NYT 12/18/15*) wrote that contemporary
science has refined the old "fight or flight" concept — the idea that these are the
two hard-wired options when in mortal danger needs updating to:

- "Freeze
- Flee
- Fight"

While "freeze, flee, fight" is superficially like "run, hide, fight", the two
expressions make fundamentally different assumptions about how and why
we do what we do when in danger. Ledoux reports on the psychological
research studies showing that if people can cognitively reappraise a situation,
they can dampen their amygdale activity that causes them to freeze. This
dampening may open the way for conceptually based actions, like "run, hide,
fight," to replace freezing and other hard-wired impulses.... or, at least, reduce
the freezing time and hasten our coming to our senses.

Three legs make up the U.S. nuclear triad:

- Strategic bombers
- Submarine-launched ballistic missiles (SLBMs)
- Intercontinental ballistic missiles (ICBMs).

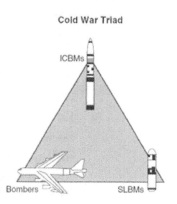

Cold War Triad

Each component complements the force as a whole by
providing distinct capabilities. This is from a paper by
Constance Baroudos of the Lexington Institute called, "A
Nuclear Triad Is Far Superior To A Dyad Or Monad"
(5/18/2015 at their website at lexingtoninstitute.org.) The
nuclear deterrent causes potential enemies to recognize
that their eventual loss will exceed any gain that could
result from launching a nuclear attack on America or its
allies. Each component of the triad complements the
ensemble by providing distinct capabilities. Yeehaw
Yahoo! USA USA USA!

Besides the big threats like active shooters or crazy politicians, Oren Jay Sofer points out that our billion-year-old biology kicks in whenever we make eye contact by asking:

- Is it friend?
- Is it foe?
- Is it a mate?

(His book is say what you mean)

The Party of Socialism and Liberation promotes this slogan:

- Trump is the symptom
- Capitalism is the disease
- Socialism is the cure.

In Sociology for Dummies, Jay Gabler defines sociology as the scientific study of society. The field was founded by a power trio, whose ideas are still prominent to this day:

- Karl Marx (1818-1883) - a German philosopher who believed that material goods are at the root of the social world. According to Marx, social life is fundamentally about the conflict over food, land, money, and other material goods.
- Emile Durkheim (1858-1917) - a French sociologist who argued that society had to be studied on its own terms — that understanding individual psychology was insufficient. He believed that societies are held together by shared values that are always changing. (A group of people is like a sea of floating magnets which can be calm or stormy)
- Max Weber (1864-1920) - a German sociologist who agreed with Marx that people often fight to protect their own interests. He also agreed with Durkheim that what people consider their interests often are determined by socialization and shared values; and these days, I think, by various media channels saturating the people's consciousnesses.

Ken Wilber's three strands of a valid knowledge quest:

- Injunction to do the practice
- Illumination gained from having practiced
- Confirmation of results within the peer group of practitioners, as when the believer testifies.

This parallels the scientific quest:

- Do an experiment to measure an aspect of the physical world
- Verify or not a proposed law of nature
- Publish the results in a peer-reviewed journal.

from the Charlie Chaplin movie "Modern Times"

To consolidate his dictatorship, Hitler abolished the independent unions in Germany in a single blow. Trump faced no such problems. In the first three postwar decades, workers and management effectively shared the increased wealth produced by the growth of productivity. Since the 1970s:

- That social contract has collapsed
- Union membership and influence have declined
- Inequality in wealth has increased

"The Suffocation of Democracy" by Christopher R. Browning in The New York Review of Books (10/25/2018)

People have various admixtures of three primary constitutions according to the Ayurvedic system of medicine.

- *Kapha*   water and earth elements predominate. These types will typically have a solid bodily frame and calm temperament
- *Pitta*   fire and water elements predominate. These types will tend to have a fiery personality and oily skin
- *Vata*   air and ether elements predominate. These types are commonly quick thinking, thin, and fast moving.

http://www.eattasteheal.com/ayurveda101/eth_bodytypes.htm

Rudy Ballentine's three things that contribute to radical healing:
- Nutrition
- Exercise
- Cleansing

Ballentine is an MD. Two of his books are <u>Radical Healing</u> and <u>Diet and Nutrition.</u>

Swami Chinmayananda's triadic tripling of sight, seer and seen:
- Perceiving-thinking-feeling
- Body-mind-intellect
- Object-thought-emotion

The Swami, who died in 1993, was a Hindu spiritual leader and teacher who left behind many writings and the Chinmaya Mission. Here are three quotes from his work:
- "To deny a thought is to engage a thought. Leave it alone - Let it pass."
- "The tragedy of human history is that there is decreasing happiness in the midst of increasing comforts."
- "Disappointment can come only to those who make an appointment with the future."

Three aspects of the absolute
- Existence
- Knowledge
- Bliss.

called *Sat, Chit, and Ananda* in the Indian scriptures. Ramana Maharshi said, "The whole universe is but a tiny ripple on the infinite ocean of Sat-Chit-Ananda." Rupert Spira's modern take on this aphorism is "The knowing of our own being is happiness itself." He says that this knowing is awareness. (See him on outube.com and also his book, <u>Being Aware of Being Aware</u>)

The three numbers of modern cosmology describing the state of the universe:
- Age of the universe
- Mass of the universe
- Rate at which the universe is expanding

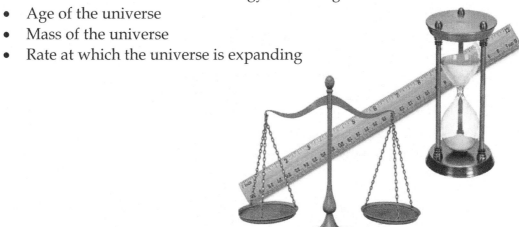

The three measurables of classical physics:
- Mass with the Planck mass $= 2.176\,51(13) \times 10^{-8}$ <u>kilograms</u>
- Length with the Planck length $= 1.616\,199(97) \times 10^{-35}$ meters
- Time with the Planck time $= 5.391\,06(32) \times 10^{-44}$ second

Measurements of mass, length, and time are usually expressed in standard units such as kilograms, meters, and seconds. These are man-made units, not intrinsically tied to the physics of basic reality, but to such things as the weight of stones, the length of a king's arm, and the time for a heart to beat. In fundamental units, called Planck units, the fundamental parameters such as Planck's constant, the speed of light, and Newton's universal constant of gravitation are all equal to one. Carlo Rovelli, in his book, <u>Reality Is Not What It Seems,</u> writes about Matvei Bronŝtejn, a young Soviet physicist killed by Stalin. He was the first to calculate the Plank length as the distance small enough at which an elementary particle collapses into a black hole. Rovelli invokes the John Wheeler metaphor that the ocean looks smooth from a cruising airplane but looks ruffled by waves and foam lower down. Just so is space-time near the Plank length. Oh! It's also good realize that the size of the atomic nucleus is closer to the human size than it is to the Plank length; a trillionth of a trillionth of a trillionth of a meter.

A questioner asked Ramana if there is a God apart from ourselves. Ramana answered, "If by 'ourselves' you mean your body, then there is a creator. If you objectify and see a universe, then you are bound to see many things besides yourself:

- Body,
- God, and
- World

rise and set together from and into the Self." Ramana taught that we should always be asking the question, "Who Am I? " and the asking is not to be done with words or with the mind but with our whole being!

I am not what I consume, think, vote for, do ...

What about "me?", a voice asked when I approached a deep meditation. If I'm not 'me' than who am I?" Modern *advaita* teacher, Rupert Spira, in his youtube talk, "See Clearly Who You Are" defines consciousness or awareness as:

See https://www.youtube.com/watch?v=U_bSnflHZ8U).

- That in which all experience appears
- That in which all experience is known
- That out of which all experience is made."

Günter Gebel-Williams was the greatest performer of all time in the Ringling Brothers, Barnum and Bailey three-ring circus.

- In the center ring, he was the lion tamer who worked and communicated with big cats of all kinds.
- In the left ring, he worked with a team of horses.
- In the right ring, he worked with his beloved elephants.

In his financial blog of late 2017, John Hussman examines the anatomy of speculative bubbles and discusses three popular delusions that have taken hold of the crowd:

- Delusion of paper wealth
- Delusion of a booming economy
- Delusion that is Bitcoin.

In How Fascism Works; Jason Stanley shows that fascist politics "seek to undermine public discourse by attacking and devaluing:

- Education,
- Expertise, and
- Language."

Later (NYT 7/3/2019), he wrote, "Liberal democracy organizes society around respect for the

- dignity,
- equality and
- freedom

of all human beings. Fascism, by contrast, organizes society around the vilification of outsiders." He points out that with Trump's vilification of outsiders, "we have been subject to classic fascist tropes". He points out that Hitler admired America's immigration-policies.

The consorts of the male Gods of the Hindu Trinity:

- Saraswati   Goddess of Wisdom
- Lakshmi   Goddess of Wealth
- Parvati   Goddess of the Mountain.

The signature triad of Western culture according to Leonard Shlain:

- Law codes
- Dualistic philosophy
- Objective science.

Two of Shlain's great books are <u>The Alphabet Versus the Goddess: The Conflict Between Word and Image</u> and <u>Sex, Time and Power: How Women's Sexuality Shaped Human Evolution.</u>

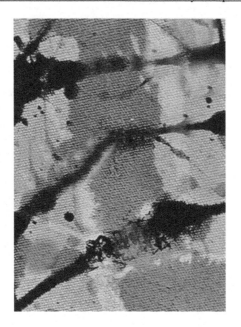

Eckhart Tolle's three ways to practice the power of Now:

- Watch the thought
- Feel the emotion
- Observe the reaction.

The Andrews Sisters, three ladies who entertained the troops during WWII:

- Laverne
- Maxine
- Shirley.

(see Andrews Sisters "Boogie Woogie Bugle Boy" on youtube.com)

Three prime factors for attaining the highest in life:
- Association with the wise
- Divine grace
- Dispassion

as stated by the sage Dattatreya in the *Tripuri Rahasya*, an ancient work whose title means "The Mystery beyond the Three Cities, which are the three states of consciousness: wakefulness, dreaming, and deep sleep.

Ken Wilber's big three:
- "I"
- "We"
- "It"

Newton's and Shakespeare's triadic conception of time:
- Past
- Present
- Future

is old fashioned now that Einstein showed, in his theory of relativity of 1905, that it follows from the constancy of the speed of light, that two events that are simultaneous for one observer occur sequentially in time for another. Bill, on the platform sees two lightning bolts hit two poles equidistant from him at the same time (simultaneously). An observer, Alice, on a moving train passing by the platform sees the bolt that hits the pole toward which the train is moving hit before the bolt that hits the other pole. This is because the light coming from this other (moving-away from) pole must catch up to the train, travels a longer distance, and takes more time to travel to the observer on the train. The light striking the first pole has less distance to travel and thus takes less time. By relativity theory, the speed of light is the same for all observers and one observer is not privileged over the other, especially if they are on two passing ships at sea on a dark night or on two passing spaceships in intergalactic space.

The past, present and future walk into a bar. It was tense.

Three tenets of realism:
- Things exist
- They have properties
- They have causes and effects.
  lecture by Terry Rudolph https://www.youtube.com/watch?v=JKGZDhQoR9E

The three elemental forces with which the emperor Marcus Aurelius identified himself:
- Providence
- Necessity
- Nature

The three temporal states of the human mind as stated in the Mandukya Upanishad:
- Recollection
- Awareness
- Anticipation

which are concerned respectively with past deeds, experience of the now, and present desires.

Plato's big three:
- Truth
- Goodness
- Beauty

The biggest complaints in modern society are by people being:
- Overscheduled
- Overcommitted
- Overextended.   Kate Murphy, NYT July 25, 2014

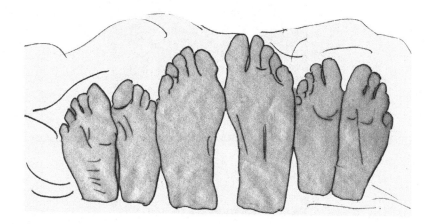

Three realms of *samsaric* existence (the cycles of birth, death, and rebirth) of living creatures:
- Realm of Desire
- Realm of Form
- Realm of Non-Form.

Eckhart Tolle gives three options for taking responsibility and for maintaining your presence and consciousness in the Now when dealing with a negative situation:

- Speak out, change the situation
- Accept the situation, surrender
- Leave the situation

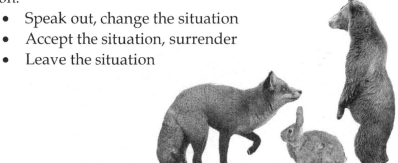

The "Brers Three" found in the tales of Uncle Remus:

- Brer Fox who jabbered away like a blue jay on amphetamine
- Brer Rabbit whose slick cunning discourse always seemed to outfox the fox
- Brer Bear who lumbered along and said, "I'm gonna knock hiz head clean off"

Their symbolic significance is very subtle, profound, and mysterious. *These characters were featured in the 1946 Walt Disney Movie, "Song of the South" that is no longer considered politically correct because it mixed the daintiness of a plantation life with a slavery absent of its horror; the life of slaves in brutal forced labor camps.* Another important character in the movie was the Tar Baby 'cause he didn't say "nuffin."

Republican political operative, Dick Army said, "Three groups spend other people's money:

- Children
- Thieves
- Politicians"

All three need supervision.

The three fishermen from the children's bedtime story:
- Winkin'
- Blinkin'
- Nod.

from Johnson's first-(fifth) reader   1899

A triad of mental functioning:
- Thought
- Word
- Meaning.

The central triune structure of information in Albert Borgman's paradigm:
- Thing
- Person
- Sign

in which the person is informed by the sign about the thing. His book is, <u>Holding On to Reality: The Nature of Information at the Turn of the Millennium.</u>

The "Big Three" who formulated the world order for the latter half of the twentieth century at Yalta:

- Churchill
- Roosevelt
- Stalin

Three schools of thought about teaching and learning:

- Cognitive School of Thought - brain based learning,
- Humanistic School of Thought - suggests that learning improves in a classroom that is more humane and when the school is made to fit the child
- Behavioral School of Thought - learning is accomplished best when teachers know how to utilize the learning environment to encourage learning.

https://studentteachingtools.weebly.com/3-schools-of-thought-about-teaching-and-learning.htm

"...isn't placing ourselves in the cradle of nature the very action that makes us physically and emotionally

- Complete
- Composed
- Content?"

Where circumstances limit or deprive us of the opportunity, don't we pine to once again be in the sanctum of creation with the:

- Majesty of the mountains
- Sublimity of the sea
- Dichotomy of the desert

These elements evoke the same feelings in us as they did for ancestral generations, people who were well pleased to be living with the land, not merely living on it." Greg Lawson wrote these words in the forward to his photographic masterpiece, <u>California in the Beginning</u>.

When suffering people come to a saint for the relief of their condition, the saint can do the following:

- Remove the problem
- Reduce the severity of the problem
- Impart acceptance of the problem

The three states of consciousness:

- Waking
- Dream
- Deep sleep

are presided over by *Tripurasundari*, the Goddess of the Three Cities.

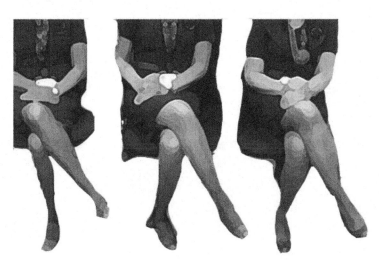

The threefold Vedic activity of the mind:

- Ascertainment of sense objects
- Appropriation to one's self (egoism)
- Thought constructs about sense objects.

The three possible fundamental mathematical relationships between any two numbers:

- **X > Y**   greater than
- **X = Y**   equal to
- **X < Y**   less than.

In <u>A World of Three Zeros</u>, Muhammad Yunus describes the new economics emerging from the dysfunction of modern capitalism, a world of:

- Zero Poverty
- Zero Unemployment
- Zero Net Carbon Emissions

Kant's three critiques:

- Pure Reason
- Practical Reason
- Aesthetic Judgment

Vasishta, one of the sages who created the Rig Veda, extolled a threefold root of self-effort:
- Knowledge of the scriptures
- Instructions of the guru
- Self-effort

Vasishtha's threefold fruit of self-effort:
- An inner awakening in the intelligence
- A decision in the mind
- The physical action

Vasishtha also appears in the Ramayana (a favorite scripture of right-wing Hindus) as the teacher of Rama. In Modi's India of 2019, "*Jay Sri Ram*" is being used as a call for murder by wild Hindu mobs. By contrast, in the USA, the gangster president's chants of "Build the Wall" have not moved mobs to murder yet, only crazed lone-wolf alt-right armed to the hilt active shooters have been so moved by his rhetoric.

Three reasons given by **S**lavoy Zizek in his book <u>Zizek's Jokes</u> by which we can be sure that Jesus was Jewish:
- He took up his father's profession
- His mother thought he was God
- He couldn't imagine his parents had sexual relations

The ancient Egyptian trinity of:
- Isis
- Osiris
- Horus

In the myth from 2400 BC, Osiris is murdered by his brother, Set, who usurps his throne, but Isis, Osiris's queen, restores her husband's body and manages to have him conceive a son, Horus, with her. Horus then grows up to triumph over Set and complete the resurrection of Osiris.

The three experiences which neurotic St. Augustine misinterpreted and misunderstood:
- Birth
- Sexuality
- Mortality

Thereby, he really screwed up Western civilization for several millennia.
(See David G. Hunter, Sex, Sin and Salvation: What Augustine Really Said
http://www.jknirp.com/aug3.htm)

Tinker to Evers to Chance - the famous double-play combination of the Chicago Cubs in the early part of the twentieth century:
- Joe Tinker - shortstop
- Johnny Evers - second baseman
- Frank Chance - first baseman

All three were inducted into Baseball's Hall of Fame.

Three types of yoga:
- *Karma yoga*, path of doing good work of selfless service; for example, the folks at "Doctors Without Borders"
- *Jnana yoga*, path of knowledge; foremost is the Oneness teacher Ramana Maharshi
- *Bhakti yoga*, path of the heart, like the devotion, prayer, and singing of Mahalia Jackson or Mata Amritananda Devi

The teachers say, that all paths merge at the "mountain top."

Eduardo Galeano points out that the powers of Europe prepared for war against the French Revolution because it insulted and threatened the holy trinity of:
- Crown
- Wig
- Cassock   *his book is <u>Mirrors</u>*

In <u>The Meaning of Human Existence</u>, Edward O. Wilson quotes the Stoic Roman philosopher, Seneca the Younger, "Religion is regarded by:
- The common people as true
- The wise as false
- The rulers as useful

The three medieval estates:
- Nobility
- Clergy
- Commoners

Peace Pilgrim was a *sadhu* who said, "I deal with spiritual truth which
- Should never be sold,
- Need never be bought,
- When you are ready it will be given"

She began her pilgrimage during the Korean War when she changed her name from Mildred Norman to the name emblazoned on her distinctive tunic, PEACE PILGRIM. She walked in the Rose Bowl parade of 1953 and kept on walking non-stop for 28 years
- "I own only what I wear and carry.
- I just walk until given shelter,
- fast until given food,"

she said; "I don't even ask; it's given without asking. I tell you, people are good. There's a spark of good in everybody." She walked for World Peace.

The ego's unholy trinity as expressed in <u>A Course in Miracles</u>:
- Sin
- Guilt
- Fear

<u>A Course in Miracles</u> is a modern Oneness teaching channeled through the clinical research psychologist, Helen Schuman, who never claimed any credit of authorship during her lifetime. Its main character is Jesus, the inner guru, who helps students get past avalanches, storms and foggy weather caused by the ego's battle with the Oneness of Reality. The ego says to Jesus, "I'm Me, now get your ass out of here!" What Jesus says to the ego are the teachings of "The Course", the main one is that "a miracle is a change of perception leading towards Oneness."

The code of Hammurabi distinguishes three classes of people:

- Superiors
- Commoners
- Slaves

Yuval Harari pointed out that the code gives explicit punishments for a person who puts out an eye or kills a member of each of these classes. The values of the punishments vary considerably ... very different and perhaps less harsh then justice meted out in the American justice system to members of some racial castes. (Does the Code of Hammurabi mention castration or lynching?) Harari wrote that both the Code of Hammurabi and the American Declaration of Independence are man-made fabrications not created or handed down by gods or coming from any sort of natural law. How could men be "created" equal, Harari asks, when they "evolved" and were not "created" - these two documents are part of the fabric of an "Imaginary Order."   *(see Sapiens)*

Edward O. Wilson posits three levels of biodiversity in his book, The Meaning of Human Existence:

- Top-level of ecosystems such as meadows, lakes, and coral reefs
- Species that make up each ecosystem
- Genes that prescribe the distinguishing traits of each species

Eduardo Galeano has a vignette in <u>Mirrors</u> about the origin of social classes. The sun's rays penetrated a woman who instantly gave birth to a baby. The god, *Panchacamac*, was not pleased and tore the baby into pieces. From these pieces of the dead infant came the first plants. The sun was furious and blasted the coast of Peru leaving it forever dry. As further revenge, the sun placed three eggs on the soil:

- From the golden egg emerged the lords,
- From the silver egg came the ladies of the lords, and
- From the copper egg came the ones who do the work.

The Jewish religion has three veins flowing through it:

- Crazy -   the Orthodox branch of the faith
- Hazy -   the Conservative branch of the faith
- Lazy -   the Reform branch of the faith

The Orthodox try to stick to the letter of the law as God wrote it in the holy scriptures. They keep kosher and don't ride or turn on the lights on the Sabbath. They don't stone adulterous ladies anymore. Some of them wear 17th-century Polish style clothing and some wear wide hats. The Reform try to be modern and secular in outlook. The conservatives are betwixt and between. They all read the holy Torah scroll through communally once per year, portion by weekly portion. A *bar mitzvah* ritual is included once in a while providing a party after the Sabbath service... (see Rabbi Mark B. Greenspan http://www.oceansidejewishcenter.org/rebmark/Pre2002/ravms5.html)

The three sons of Adam and Eve:
- Cain
- Able
- Seth

Spiritual teacher, Tara Brach, has a video on youtube.com called, "Three Gestures of Love", in which she references the teaching and healing practice of Hawaiian master, Ihaleakala Dr. Hew Len, who works in the tradition of Ho'oponopono. Tara Brach says the healing of a relationship or situation with yourself or with others is done by evoking the three-fold mantra:
- I'm sorry
- I love you
- Thank you.

She says "I'm sorry" evokes compassion and forgiveness. One formulation of this Ho'oponopono cleansing mantra is: I'm sorry, forgive me, I love you, and thank you. The recipe is stir and repeat again and again throughout your life and do this for both negative and positive situations. "The only task in your life and mine is the restoration of our Identities ~ our Minds ~ back to their original state of void or zero," says Ihaleakala Hew Len, Ph.D. The cleansing brings you back to the state of zero or Oneness.

Wendy Doniger's book, <u>Hindus</u>, was banned in India after a right-wing Hindu fundamentalist brought a suit against Penguin Books. The book posits that three animals "are particularly charismatic players in the drama of Hinduism:

- Horses
- Dogs
- Cows

because the ancient texts use them to symbolize:

- Power
- Pollution
- Purity

They thus represent the castes of the warriors, the low-born, and the Brahmins. Left out of this scheme are the merchants who are included in the category of the twice born; those who have a spiritual birth as well as a body birth. These people are:

- Brahmins, the priestly caste
- *Kshatriyas.* the warrior caste
- *Vaishyas*, the merchant caste

All of which brings on the age-old debate as to whether caste should be determined by birth or by the quality of the individual and if, over the centuries, caste consciousness arose as an aberration of the original society. "If by birth" means you are a member of the caste in which you are born. "If by quality" means that brahmins are the people who are smart in school; they are the intellectuals. The *kshatriyas* are the athletes in high school and later become the warriors. The *vaishyas* are practical-minded people. Below them are the *sudras* who form the working class. It's convoluted by now. Caste can also imply trade-guild and it pretty much goes by birth as we see in the West with people having last names like Taylor, Carpenter, and Brewer. Also underlying the whole system, it seems to me, is the tribalistic racism that the light-skinned conquering Vedic people had for the indigenous darker skinned people of the Indian subcontinent.

The Harvard Medical School website posted an article by David Cameron in August 2013 titled "Genetics Proves Indian Population Mixture." The study, done by scientists from Harvard Medical School and from CSIR-Centre for Cellular and Molecular Biology in Hyderabad, India, posits two major ancestral populations in India: Ancestral North Indians (ANI), who are related to Central Asians, Middle Easterners, Caucasians, and Europeans; and Ancestral South Indians (ASI), who are primarily from the subcontinent. "The researchers studying a pool of 73 Indian population groups took advantage of the fact that the genomes of Indian people are a mosaic mixture of chromosomal segments of ANI and ASI descent. "Originally when the ANI and ASI populations mixed, these segments would have been extremely long, extending the entire lengths of chromosomes. However, after mixture these segments would have broken up at one or two places per chromosome, per generation, recombining the maternal and paternal genetic material that occurs during the production of egg and sperm." "This genetic data tell us a three-part cultural and historical story," said David Reich, professor of genetics at Harvard Medical School:

- Prior to about 4000 years ago there was no mixture.
- Between 4000 and 2000 years ago widespread mixture affected almost every group in India, even the most isolated tribal groups.
- Then the caste system's endogamy set in and "froze everything in place"

Plato advanced a caste system as well in his utopian Republic, where society would be composed of:

- Philosopher kings
- Warriors or protectors
- Producers – farmers and craftsmen

This is different from the Hindu system in which the Brahmins on the top of the totem pole are priests who wave lights around the fire, pour ghee into the fire to bring up the flame, throw drops of water around and shower flower petals on images of the deity, all in a very concentrated, prescribed manner accompanied by various *mudras* or hand gestures as they chant the ancient mantras,

The Greek philosophers, on the western side of Eurasia, sat around in their togas thinking thoughts and diddlin' the young boys. When Rome fell, the philosopher kings became priests as the empire became the church and they are still diddlin'...so goes the theory of Gilbert Webb, a wise man of South Carolina.

Going down the totem pole, the Indian warrior class had the political power, but the Greek warriors took orders from above. Finally, Plato had no businessmen in his system, just pure producers with no middlemen. Plato couldn't have made it in the today's capitalistic culture unless he stayed in a cloister or in a one-percenter's gated community, wearing his white toga, and giving classes and private sessions in New Age happy horse whinny.

The three fires whose maintenance was the responsibility of every Vedic householder:
* *Garhapatya*, the household fire
* *Dakshine*, the ceremonial fire
* *Ahavaniya*, the sacrificial fire

Wendy Doniger

Ram Das compares the views of old age and death in traditional India and in today's modern global world culture. In the first, there is an emphasis on the eternal, and thus relief of suffering as well as not fighting against nature because the goal is reaching God, rather than in the second case, obtaining:
* Thin thighs
* Fabulous pensions
* Geriatric erections.

An ignorant stereotype of the Hindu culture is that it consists of the 3 C's:
* Caste
* Cows
* Curry *Wendy Doniger*

Three respectively more subtle individualized Hindu spiritual practices:
* Puja, which is done by waving lights around fire, dropping flower pedals, burning incense, throwing drops of water, and by chanting mantras before the image of the deity in a state of concentration.
* Japa that uses the words and sounds of mantras in a state of concentration
* Meditation bringing one into states of inner concentrated awareness

from the wealth of Wendy Doninger's book, <u>Hindus</u>

The three tigers that the young sage, Little Black Sambo, watched as they turned into butter:

- The tiger of thought
- The tiger of word
- The tiger of meaning

He was great because he was a little kid who wasn't scared by the tigers and didn't cry when they took his clothes. He climbed the tree to safety, and calmly watched them destroy themselves as they ran around and around the tree chasing each other trying to get a better piece of clothing, only to merge into a big puddle of butter with Sambo's clothes neatly separated out. Such is my childhood memory of my experience with the story. He was a hero to me not a denigrated member of a lower race of beings.

In the early days of the internet, there was a bulletin board where people of considerable intellect debated the racism inherent in the story. Out of that discussion, several versions of the story were later published:

- One version is set in India,
- One version, by Julius Lester, called <u>Sam and the Tigers</u>, is set in Black Chicago
- One version simply changed the name from Little Black Sambo to Little White Mary.

Presence, wrote Oren Jay Sofer, despite the difficulty of capturing it with language, is "the experience of being fully aware and sensing one's body in the present moment." Presence, he writes, is embodied awareness of our

- direct sensory experience
- our direct mental experience
- our direct emotional experience

In <u>say what you mean,</u> he writes about a mindful approach to nonviolent communication.

What every warrior needs:
- Sword
- Shield
- Helmet

Julius Caesar's famous line in a letter he wrote to the Roman Senate after the Battle of Zela in 46 B.C. as given by Wikipedia: "veni, vidi, vici" =

- I came
- I saw
- I conquered

It's a very popular logo for tattoos these days.

Listen to Ella Fitzgerald sing the song
- "Bewitched
- Bothered
- Bewildered"

It was composed by Richard Rodgers in 1940 for the Broadway show, Pal Joey. Ella made her version on the album Ella Fitzgerald Sings the Rodgers & Hart Songbook (1956). Wikipedia lists 45 other recordings of the song in a list of the most popular singers of the 20th and early 21st centuries. Ella is so convincing when she sings the last two verses:

Men are not a new sensation
I've done pretty well I think
But this half-pint imitation
Put me on the blink
I've sinned a lot
I'm mean a lot
But now I'm like seventeen a lot
Bewitched, bothered, and bewildered am I.

What a voice, beautiful, hip, full, strong, and soft... this is classic Americana.

Three fundamental types of information according to Albert Borgman:
- Natural information as when dark clouds indicate rain or when a gravel bed or line of cottonwood trees indicates the presence of a river.
- Cultural or conventional signs that point to something "real" such as a cairn of piled up stones, or a treaty, covenant, construction plan, or written score for a cantata.
- Technological information as in digital music or in a video game that presents its own virtual reality.

See Borgman's book <u>*Holding On to Reality: The Nature of Information at the Turn of the Millennium*</u>

Jean Klein speaks of relatedness in his book, <u>Who Am I - The Sacred Quest.</u> We, must first know and love ourselves, he wrote, before we can:

- Understand others
- Love others
- Welcome others

He wrote that we must first do a "thorough reading of our own book" to know our reactions, resistances, tensions, emotional states, and so on. This reading involves no special system or set of exercises but demands that "we face ourselves during the day without habitual identification, without an individual center of reference, an I-image, a personality, or a propagator of viewpoints." To do this scientifically, we must "accept the facts as they are without:

- Agreement
- Disagreement
- Conclusion

The three phases of medical healing:

- Diagnosis
- Prognosis
- Treatment

Wikipedia defines "hendiatris" as a figure of speech employed for emphasis, in which three words are used to express one idea. In Shakespeare, we find:

- "Cry God for Harry, England, and St. George" (*Henry V*)
- "Friends, Romans, countrymen, lend me your ears" (*Julius Caesar*)
- "Be bloody, bold, and resolute" (*Macbeth*).

In the U.S. Constitution, we see: "Life, Liberty, and the Pursuit of Happiness." A famous Nazi slogan during the Third Reich was: "Ein Volk! Ein Reich! Ein Führer" used by Hitler in the 1934 Nuremberg rally of a million people. At the same time, the Italian mobs shouted "Believe, obey, fight", at Mussolini's rallies. Modern Germany inscribes upon its Euro coins: "Unity and Justice and Freedom." Every Tom, Dick, and Harry" in the environmental movement knows the slogan: "Reduce, Reuse, Recycle." And one we all know is:

- Wine
- Women
- Song

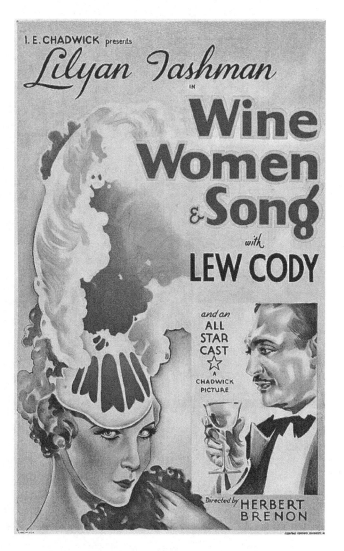

The list goes on: "God, mother, and apple pie", "Lock, stock, and barrel", "Hamburger, French fries, and a Coke", "Healthy, wealthy and wise" and "Signed, sealed, delivered."

Automated warfare is coming with its smart decision-making machines. "Don't Let Bots Pull the Trigger" is the title the editors of "Scientific American" give their article in the March 2019 issue. They ask an important question. "After the battle is over, who will be held responsible when a machine automatically does the killing:

- The robot
- Its owner
- Its maker?"

They are not just mobile machine guns equipped with cameras and decision-making A.I neural networks. There could be swarms of very small inexpensive weaponized smart drones released by terrorists on population centers. The editors are calling for an international ban on such weapons just as there are bans for nuclear and chemical weapons.

The Parable of the Rich Fool is found in Luke 12 :18 "Then he said, 'This is what I will do: I will tear down my barns and build larger ones, and there I will store all my grain and my goods. 12:19 "And I will say to my soul, "Soul, you have many goods laid up for many years to come; take your ease":

- Eat
- Drink
- Be merry.

12:20 "But God said to him, 'You fool! This very night your soul is required of you, and now who will own what you have prepared?"

Makes you wonder how in the most religious country in the modern West, people in the capital of political power have prayer breakfasts and continually make efforts to increase the stores of wealth for themselves and for their donors at the expense of people on the earth and the Earth itself. With a base of Evangelicals, the clown president is the barker out in front of the government tent, while inside, a sideshow of horrors goes on.

A three course meal:
- soup or salad
- entrée
- dessert

The famous triple in the "Rubaiyat" of Omar Khayyam, in the translation of Edward FitzGerald:
- A loaf of bread beneath the bough
- A flask of wine
- Thou

It has a double meaning elucidated by Paramahansa Yogananda. In his book commenting on the poem, <u>Wine of the Mystic</u>, Yogananda pointed out that Omar Khayyam was a highly evolved Sufi. He reads the above as

"Sitting in the deep silence of meditation, with my mind concentrated on the cerebrospinal tree of life and spiritual consciousness, I rest in the shade of peace. Nourished by the life-giving 'bread' of prana [life energy], I quaff the aged wine of divine intoxication brimming the cask of my soul.
(See the website of the Self Realization Fellowship)

Yogananda said, "One day as I was deeply concentrated on the pages of Omar Khayyam's "Rubaiyat", I suddenly beheld the walls of its outer meanings crumble away, and the vast inner fortress of golden spiritual treasures stood open to my gaze."

The Three-Body Problem is an outstanding, very intractable, problem in Newtonian physics which starts out when you know at a particular time (t=0) the values of the:

- Masses
- Positions
- Velocities

of three bodies and you then try to calculate, according to Newton's laws of motion, the values of these three quantities at later times. This cannot be solved in general. As of 2013, only twenty very special case solutions to the problem were known. The great 18th century mathematician-astronomer, Joseph Louis Lagrange, found five points in space, (now called Lagrange points) where a very small body in a three-body system with two large bodies would have a stable or semi-stable orbit---think of a satellite, the earth, and the sun or a satellite, the earth, and the moon. Satellites will be placed at these stable Lagrange points to form a forthcoming gravity wave telescope, an instrument not belonging to a scientist in a white lab coat, but to the whole human species.

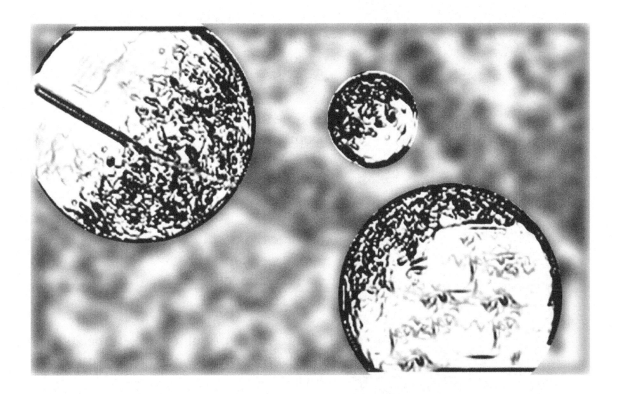

Three things by nature cause their possessor to err:)

- Youth
- Prosperity
- Ignorance.``` *Celtic triad*

Beyonce sings:
- "Me
- Myself
- I"

Thich Nhat Hanh lists three kinds of pride in which we think, I am:
- Better than others
- Worse than others
- Just as good as others

Ralph Nader (commondreams.org 9/13/15) quotes Bill Joy's article "The Future Doesn't Need Us," which warns of the oncoming converging technologies:
- Artificial intelligence
- Biotechnology
- Nanotechnology

The elements of a good popular story:
- Conflict
- Money
- Sex

The time flows in the play of a first intimate encounter:
- Before
- During
- After

The three rivers of Ireland:
- The Shannon
- The Boyne
- The Bann.

The three most popular songs of the 20th century as measured by times played on radio and television:
- "You've Lost That Lovin' Feelin'"
- "Never My Love"
- "Yesterday"

The three graces:
- Verdure
- Gladness
- Splendor

Or whatever they are called: grace, charm, beauty; Aglaia representing elegance and brightness; Thalia who stands for youth, beauty and good cheer; Euphrosyne symbolizing mirth and joyfulness. Were they the daughters of Zeus and Eurynome or the daughters of Dionysus and Aphrodite or daughters of Helios and the naiad Aegle. Antimachus didn't say what the number of the Graces was. He didn't give their names either, but he did say that they are daughters of Aegle and the Sun. The elegiac poet Hermesianax makes Persuasion also one of the Graces." Such is the mishmash from the internet. In the Greek they are called the three charities or Kharites, goddesses of grace, beauty, adornment, joy, mirth, festivity, dance and song, Great to have at a good party.

Frank Wilczek, a Nobel Prize-winning theoretical physicist, asks "a beautiful question" in his book of the same name. "Does the world embody beautiful ideas?" He notes that religious cosmologies are not concerned with Beauty. He starts at the beginning with Pythagoras whose famous theorem links concepts of number and the space of materiality. Wilczek says that when Pythagoras also discovered the laws of ratio connected to the pleasing sounds made by string instruments, he "completed a trinity:"
- Mind
- Matter
- Beauty

The Nat King Cole Trio, a classic mid-20th century group, led by a gentleman whose voice was smooth as silk, his diction as crisp as a bell and his elegance as radiant as a star. He was the first African American with his own prime time TV show which lasted only one year after the pressure from racists forced its cancelation.

The three daughters of Allah were prayed to by the pre-Islamic Arabs:

- Allat "the goddess"
- Al-Uzza "the mighty"
- Manat "the goddess of fate"

According to Reza Aslan, in his book, No god but God, these girls form the pre-Islamic Arab triple goddess. Al-Uzza, "the Strong One", the Goddess of the morning and evening star, Venus. She had a temple at Petra. Al-Lat is identified with Aphrodite by Herodotus. She was called "the Mother of the Gods", or "Greatest of All". She is a Goddess of springtime and of fertility. Manat is associated with fate, destruction, doom, and death. Don't mess with her.

Mathieu Ricard envisages a different type of economy that rests on three pillars of true prosperity:

- Nature, whose integrity we must preserve
- Human activities, which should flourish
- Financial means which ensure our survival. Mentioned in his book, Altruism.

Three temptations of Jesus:

- hedonism."
- egoism
- materialism

Peace Pilgrim encountered the same temptations as Jesus. She underwent a
- purification of her body
- purification of her thought
- purification of her desires

Then she added a fourth; purification of her motives which Jesus did by saying he was the way, the truth, and the light.

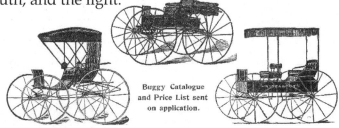

Buggy Catalogue
and Price List sent
on application.

Ramesh Balsekar's book, <u>A Duet of One,</u> begins with some sketches of the hagiography of great sages. "In the case of Zarathustra, it is said that unlike any other new-born infant, he let out not a cry but a huge laugh because he considered that life was meant to be enjoyed and not to make others unhappy:
- Good thoughts
- Good words
- Good deeds

was the essence of his teaching. "

In Gary Wills' article "Where Evangelicals Come From" (New York Review of Book 4/20/2017), he reviews <u>The Evangelicals: The Struggle to Shape America</u> by Frances FitzGerald. The article proposes three things that characterize them:
- Crowds
- Drama
- Cycles

During the first Great Awakening of the 1730s, 25,000 people were said to hear George Whitfield preach. There was a second awakening at the end of the 19th century with Billy Sunday and others. In the 20th century, Billy Graham drew big crowds and at the end of the 20th century we have mega-churches where people gather to be "slain in the spirit" with shouts of: "Amen", "Hallelujah", and "Lord Jesus." In between, there are cycles when America goes to the devil. Now, "Praise Jesus", we've elected Donald J. Trump to do the Lord's work.

Three things people can do to bring light into the world that will counteract the evil done by the terrorists in the September 11, 2001 tragedy at the World Trade Center according to an advertisement placed in the "New York Times" on September 23, 2001, by the followers of the Lubavitcher Rebbi:

- *Teshucah* - Searching our souls and correcting our behavior
- *Tefilah* - Praying to the Almighty and expressing our faith in his Divine benevolence
- *Tzedakah* - Acting more benevolently by being less judgmental and doing whatever we can to ease the emotional and material suffering of our neighbors.

The three basic themes in software paradigms for building intelligent machines, according to Kurzweil:

- Recursive searches in which a computational function calls itself. This happens when a routine to find the best chess move calls itself to find the best next move, and the best next move after that, etc.
- Self-organizing networks of elements as in massively parallel computing.
- Evolutionary improvement schemes using repeating struggle amongst competing designs.

Three Laws of Robotics were devised by the science fiction author Isaac Asimov in his 1942 short story "Runaround":

- A robot may not injure a human being, or, through inaction, allow a human being to come to harm.
- A robot must obey the orders given it by human beings, except where such orders would conflict with the First Law.
- A robot must protect its own existence as long as such protection does not conflict with the First or Second Law. (See Wikipedia or Asimov's book I Robot)

"Stuart Russell's article in "Scientific American"(*June 2016*), has a quote by Norbert Weiner warning that we must be sure of our purpose before handing authority over to smart mechanisms. Russell believes we can tackle Weiner's warning if we adhere to three core principles:

- The machine's purpose must be to maximize the realization of human values.
- The machine must be initially uncertain about what are those human values.
- The machine must be able to learn about human values by observing the choices we humans make.
  Oy Vey, Look at this world! What are the machines going to learn?

Traditional ways of living are disappearing as a new kind of structural unemployment comes about because of:

- Robotics
- Big data
- Artificial intelligence

wrote Sue Halpern in ("The Creepy New Wave of the Internet" *(New York Review of Books 11/20/2014)* There is the "internet of everything" which is estimated to "rake in $14.4 trillion by 2022 and that "will feed big data to every node—businesses, homes, vehicles—moment to moment, in real time." Halpern reviews Jeremy Rifkin's book, The Zero Marginal Cost Society: The Internet of Things, the Collaborative Commons, and the Eclipse of Capitalism. In 2015, Halpern's article," How Robots & Algorithms Are Taking Over" continues the theme with estimates of how 50% of all US jobs will be taken by the robots by 2040 including the outsourcing of programming jobs to the algorithms. In 2019, the TV ads tell how you can use an app that will choose the best possible new car for you as well as apps to choose the best possible college, and the best possible house to buy.

Oren Etzioni updates Asimov's three laws in his article, "How to Regulate Artificial Intelligence": *NYT/2/2017.*

- An A.I. system must be subject to the full gamut of laws that apply to its human operator. This rule would cover private, corporate and government systems. (We don't want A.I. to engage in cyberbullying, stock manipulation or terrorist threats.)
- An A.I. system must clearly disclose that it is not human. (A.I. systems don't just produce fake tweets; they also produce fake news videos.)
- An A.I. system cannot retain or disclose confidential information without explicit approval from the source of that information.

In <u>The Seventh Sense</u>, Joshua Cooper Ramo presents the three golden rules of computer security:

- Rule One: Do not own a computer
- Rule Two: Do not power it on
- Rule Three: Do not use it

This dictum was enunciated by Robert Morris, Sr., a cryptographic and security "genius" who held a high position at NSA in the late 20th century.

Three things upon which the world stands according to Rabbi Shimon Gamliel:

- Truth
- Peace
- Justice.

The three wise men: Melchior, Caspar, and Balthazar came bearing the gifts of gold, frankincense, and myrrh.

On a stray piece of paper found around my house, I found this gem - "If it had been three wise women instead of three wise men," the women would have:

- Asked directions and arrived on time
- Helped deliver the baby, cleaned the stable, made a casserole
- Brought practical gifts.

(http://unsourcedhumor.blogspot.com/2004/05/what-if-3-wise-men-were-women.html)

The three resources needed, according to Ray Kurzweil, to build an intelligent machine:

- Right set of formulas and algorithms.
- Knowledge base that tells you such things as the earth is the third planet from the sun and that water is wet and that fire is hot and that Michael Jordon or Lebron James was the greatest basketball player ever.
- Computational ability (200 calculations per second for the human carbon-based brain and a million times faster for circa end of the 20th-century silicon-based computers.

Here's a trilemma:

- Good
- Fast
- Cheap

You can have good and fast but then it's not cheap, or you can have fast and cheap but then it's not good.

Joshua Cooper Ramo applies this trilemma to networks as:

- Fast
- Open
- Secure;

then the network can be fast and open but not secure or it can be open and secure but then it's not fast.

Brandon Mercer wrote a newspaper article, "How Facebook Is Making Us All Dumber and Racist" in the San Francisco Chronicle, on the last day of 2015. "Orwell got it wrong in 1984. Bradbury got it wrong in Fahrenheit 451. It won't be a totalitarian government that gives us a dystopian society. It will be ourselves." Mr. Mercer wrote of the tyranny of personalization that leads to:

- Self-directed mind control
- Groupthink
- Xenophobia ("San Francisco Chronicle" 1/31/2015)

"A group that wants to win your hearts and minds doesn't need to burn books. How quaint was that? We stopped reading them long ago. " There are unnatural effects of rabid fans chattering on Facebook, Twitter, Reddit, and Tumblr, technologies that allow us to censor the information we allow into our smartphone windows on the world.

<u>Rise of the Robots</u>, a book by Martin Ford, reports on 21st-century vending machines that offer custom self-service solutions for virtually any product and make it possible to significantly reduce the three major costs to retail businesses:

- Real estate
- Labor
- Theft by customers and employees

These non-humanoid robots also offer 24/7 service and show targeted ads on their video screens while collecting credit card and other customer information. Maia Vince also points out that humans are prone to: biases, fatigue, and boredom.

Mr. Ford also quotes one of the last speeches of Dr. Martin Luther King "...a great revolution is taking place in the world today...it is a triple revolution:

- Technological revolution with the impact of automation and cybernation
- Revolution in weaponry with the emergence of atomic and nuclear weapons of warfare
- Human rights revolution with the freedom explosion that is taking place all over the world."

And there is still the voice crying through the vista of time, 'Behold, I make all things new; former things are passed away.'" Ford says that the phrase "triple revolution" referred to a report written by the Ad Hoc Committee on the Triple Revolution whose members were prominent academics, journalists, and technologists.

There are three types of karma:

- *Sanchita*   accumulated karma, either good or bad, due to our past actions either in this life or in past lives
- *Prarabdha*   karma that we are currently experiencing in the present
- *Agami*   future seeds of karma we are sowing due to our present actions in this life.

At the Cyber Security Symposium on CSPAN TV in December 2014, the panelists spoke about security risks inherent in the forthcoming internet of everything, a network where all sorts of devices are online to the internet: TV's, microwave ovens, heating systems, garden hoses, refrigerators, fish tanks, pacemakers and automobiles. The players will be:

- Consumer victims
- Criminals and law enforcement
- Government controlling all the data

The car will become the main seat for the family's internet connection. Car manufacturers will incorporate the internet computer into the one that controls the brakes and the steering, then the cybercriminals will attack, with ransomware, to stop your car or heart and not let it move or pump until you pay the ransom.

In The Master Algorithm, Pedro Domingos wrote this about machines:

- The Industrial Revolution automated manual work.
- The Information Revolution did the same for mental work.
- Machine learning automates automation itself.

He said that it's inevitable that businesses embrace machine learning because as they grow, they go through three stages:

- Owners of a mom and pop store know all their customers and what they like.
- They grow to the point that they need to hire programmers, information consultants, and database managers who generate millions of lines of code only to be gobbled by the "complexity monster."
- Then they resort to a machine learning system like the ones used by Wal-Mart, Facebook, Amazon, and Google.

"In the information-processing ecosystem," Domingos wrote, "databases, info crawlers, indexers and so on are herbivores, patiently munching on endless fields of data. Learners like statistical algorithms, online analytical processers, and so on are the predators. The predator learners eat up the fat information herbivores, digesting them and turning them into knowledge." Another triple Domingo used is the evolution from:

- Computers to
- Internet to
- Machine learners.

Moore's Law has held true about the computer revolution since the 1970s as the number of transistors on a chip have doubled approximately every two years. This has been a truly exponential explosion over generations of evolving technology.

As of the second decade of the 21st century, transistors are getting packed together in regions 14 nanometers wide, less than the size of 100 atoms of silicon. Computer operations are now being compromised by the effects of the fuzzy quantum mechanics of atomic physics. In his article, "The Search for a New Machine" (*"Scientific American", May 2015*), John Pavlus cites Hewlett-Packard engineer, Andrew Wheeler's, remark that the most expensive real estate on the planet is on the manufacturing die of a microchip where most of the transistors are used not to process but to form the storage areas for information that will be input into and retrieved from the processor. Three items, known as the memory hierarchy, are responsible for most of the problems engineers have when trying to extend the reign of Moore's law to smaller regions. These memory areas are:

- SRAM: High speed, very expensive static cache memory located on the same chip and communicating directly with the processor module. Access speeds are in the nanosecond range, billions of blinks of an eye per second.
- DRAM: More commonly known as RAM is slower and cheaper than SRAM and is located on other chips. Speeds are in the microseconds.
- Hard Drive: Memory that is not volatile like the first two and persists when the computer is turned off. It is much slower in communicating with the processor. Access speeds are in milliseconds. The research for future machines involves conflating this memory hierarchy and breaking down the memory walls.

Ramakrishna's triad: (He was a famous late 19th-century holy man living near Calcutta)
- Scripture
- Devotee
- Lord

The three Ministers of State who, upon hearing the court music, refused to fall down to worship the golden idol of Nebuchadnezzar. They were sent into the fiery furnace where they were saved by an angel of the Lord:
- Shadrach
- Meshach
- Abednego

Bertrand Russell stated three laws of logic:
- The Law of Identity: "Whatever is, is"
- The Law of Non-contradiction: "Nothing can both be and not be."
- The Law of Excluded Middle: "Everything must either be or not be." (*Law of Thought on Wikipedia*)

With lyrics like these, old Bertie could have been a rapper.

Harvard law professor, Cass Sunstein, in his book, <u>#Republic: Divided Democracy in the Age of Social Media</u>, writes about:

- Fragmentation
- Polarization
- Extremism.

As people receive their customized information feeds, providers offer more and more "personalization" in the name of consumer choice and this endangers our democracy. We need a lot more of Walter Cronkite and a lot less of Sean Hannity. Cronkite was the anchor of the evening CBS News Hour. He ended his show every evening with this saying "and that's the way it is, July 20, 1969," the day of the first moon landing and for 20 years of other days. He was a father figure that most folks believed spoke the truth. Most people in the country believed him. Hannity, on the other hand, has a show on Fox News; people must be out of their minds to believe him.

Three poisons, three objects, and three seeds of non-virtue in the *lojong* tradition, which Pema Chodron explicates as

- Passion
- Aggression
- Ignorance

determining the objects we crave, abhor, and ignore. The teaching exhorts us to not deny or reject these feelings and objects but to observe them come and go without attachment, in a state of freedom from the ego. Letting go of the three poisons and the three objects becomes the seeds of virtue.

See her book <u>This Moment Is the Perfect Teacher</u>
or go to the https://www.youtube.com/watch?v=nonzYCCjgaQ

The three core assumptions of post-modernism according to Ken Wilber:

- Reality is not given but is interpreted
- Meaning is context dependent as in the bark of the dog or tree
- The objective world is filtered through the triple lens of sign, signifier, and signified

The paradigm for 20th-century computers that were not that smart was as follows:

- Sequential Processing; execute one instruction after another sequentially (do this, do that, do the 17th step, do the 18th step... very mechanically)
- The If-Then-Else question leads to a jump in the sequence, (if debit subtract or else add) and,
- Looping; go back and do the same thing over and over again. Computers don't get bored!

There's a caveat! Remember to get the next piece of data before you go back and remember to stop when all the data is processed; otherwise, the computer goes into an endless loop! The damn things can print out a stack of paper two feet high filled with gibberish in no time. And they're accurate! If you run the same program again without fixing the mistake, the two feet of gibberish generated the second time will be exactly the same the two feet of gibberish generated the first time!

A classical Zen statement and also lyrics popularized by Donovan, a rock and roll icon in the 1960s:

- First there is a mountain
- Then there is no mountain
- Then there is.

The three primary colors:

- Red
- Blue
- Green

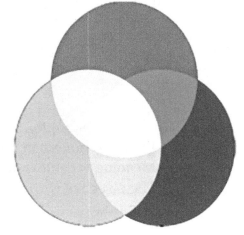

The three things that sustain the world according to the Jewish Sabbath liturgy:
- Torah
- Worship
- Loving Deeds

The Oneness teachers say the instruments of Divine guidance are:
- Directions from the mentor
- Intimations given by the soul
- Guidance from the Divine Himself or Herself

The three processes in the spiritual movement toward the Divine according to Sri Aurobindo:
- An act of self-consecration to the Divine must be made
- The seeker should learn by detachment and self-knowledge that it is God who works in him and thus he must renounce all idea of possessing existence separate from God
- The seeker must perceive all things and happenings as God

The three affirmations of the Buddhists:
- "I bow to the Buddha"
- "I bow to the *Dharma*"
- "I bow to the *Sangha*".

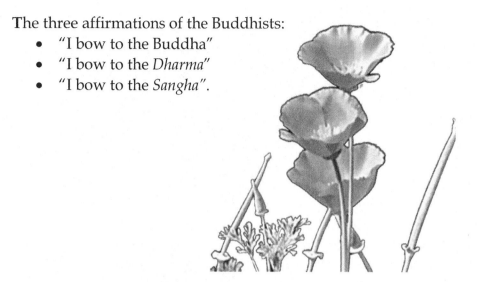

Chögyam Trungpa writes that if we have the doubt about whether or not we exist as "me," as an individual entity, or not, we become
- Baffled
- Bewildered
- Confused

and then we act out and do something like eat a piece of cake, go out on a date, fix something, clean the kitchen, get a new degree, or pull out our phones to thumb-twiddle.

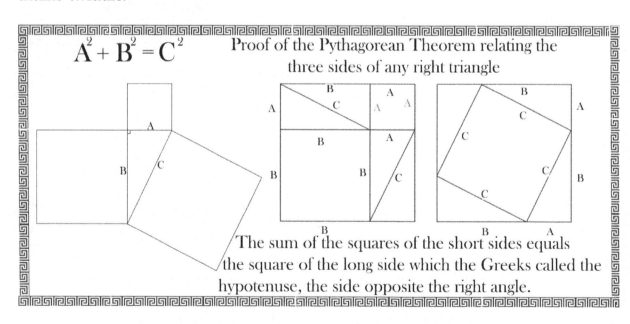

$$A^2 + B^2 = C^2$$ Proof of the Pythagorean Theorem relating the three sides of any right triangle

The sum of the squares of the short sides equals the square of the long side which the Greeks called the hypotenuse, the side opposite the right angle.

Three principals for investing in the stock market:
- Buy low, sell high.
- You can't time the market.
- Keep enough money off the table to live through the low side corrections.

The three-fold symmetry of the cantaloupe.

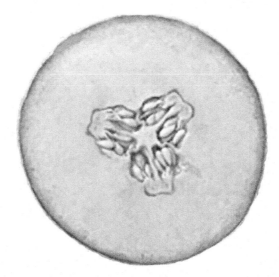

Laurence D. Fink is a founder and chief executive of Black Rock, the largest investment firm in the world. He said that his firm will have to change the ecosystem; this will mean relying more on:

- Big data
- Artificial Intelligence
- Quantified investment strategies. (Landon Thomas Jr. NYT 3/29/2017)

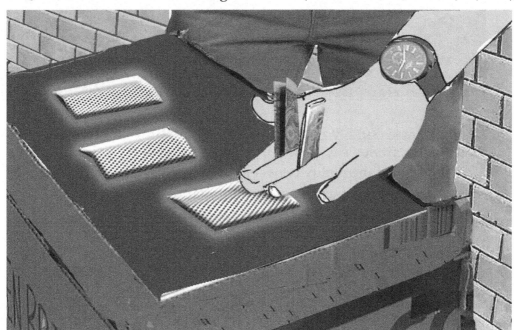

The Orwellian trinity of topsy-turvy slogans:

- War Is Peace
- Freedom Is Slavery
- Ignorance Is Strength

A slogan that appeared at the New York City Public Library on 40th St. and 5ᵗʰ Avenue after the September 11, 2001 attack on the Twin Towers:

- Recover
- Rebuild
- Remember

The Internet is Not the Answer, a book by Andrew Keen, in which he points out three major problems with the Internet:

- Increased inequality between the internet's moguls and its users
- Increased unemployment as automation mushrooms
- Increased surveillance by the national security state

Keen wrote that AI has not made people happier. It's true that anyone can post anything they want on YouTube or to their Facebook page, but they are giving away the fruits of their labor while the Larry Pages and Mark Zuckerbergs reap all the profits. Keen notes that the internet was created by relatively unknown scientists and engineers tinkering with the publicly funded ARPANET and the early internet. It's upon their labor and the infrastructure and the atmosphere they created that the gadgets of Steve Jobs' Apple and the services of Jeff Bezos' Amazon have flourished. These new guys have just put addictive cherries on top of a detailed multilayered caked that's been baked in the oven since the mid-20th century creations of transistors and von Neumann computers.

In politics, the voter knows best. In business, the customer is always right. Personal freedom is a human right goes the story of Liberalism. The Liberal story, even though it may be on the ropes in 2019, "cherishes human liberty as its number one value", writes Yuval Harari in 21 Lessons for the 21st Century. Liberalism asserts that all authority ultimately comes from the free will of individuals as expressed by their:

- feelings
- desires
- choices

This is a Liberalism that would have been endorsed by Ronald Reagan who said, "government is the problem" and Margaret Thatcher who said, " ...there is no such thing as society. There are individual men and women, and there are families." So when it comes to the extremely complicated decision of whether or not England should leave the European Union, a election was called to measure the feelings, desires, and choices of the citizens.

The Presence bridges the timeless and the illusory sense of perception. The three interruptions to this Presence are:

- Living in a state of expectation
- Living in a state of motivation
- Living in a state of interpretation.

This according to Tony Parsons in his book, As It Is

The three beasts from which Dante fled during his journey through life:
- The Leopard, representing worldly pleasure or the city of Florence
- The Lion, symbolizing pride or the Royal House of France
- The Wolf, signifying pride of the Papal See.

"Two Truths and a Lie" is a party game for teenagers and any sort of group that wants to break the ice. I'll go first, you guess the lie:
- I had a close encounter with a huge brown bear in Yosemite National Park
- I always watch Seinfeld
- I served a pitcher of iced tea to the guests into which I had mistakenly poured salt instead of sugar

Joel, an old guy in a men's group, said that he was giving up:
- Righteous indignation
- Immortality
- Improving himself

Three methods Robert Adams gives for the path to self-realization: (see his book of dialogues, Silence of the Heart, and note that his talks and writings are all online)

- Surrender completely to God
- Constant practice of mindfulness
- Constant practice of Self-Inquiry (Who am I?)

"How important is nutrition?", asked a seeker of the Oneness teacher? Jean Klein responded, "Your body is what you:

- Think
- Feel
- Eat."

Food is not only what you take in through the mouth but also what comes from your interactions with all the energies in your environment. Jean Klein wrote that meditation is a sequence of moments of:

- Grace
- Peace
- Letting go

Klein also said that the same object can at different times produce:

- Joy
- Disgust
- Complete indifference

This goes to prove that the object does not produce joy; it is merely the trigger that sets off the emotion. See his book Be What You Are.

An exemplar of 1940's jitterbug music, Louis Jordan, sang, "Whenever I go to a dance, you never see me takin' a chance. I get a kick 'cause the chicks that I pick come just:

- Slender
- Tender
- Tall.

The Celtic trinity of women:

- Maiden
- Mother
- Crone

Jean Klein taught his students yoga, beginning with a conviction that there's nothing to achieve and as a way to become acquainted with what we take for granted as:

- Body
- Senses
- Mind

"First we come to know what we are not," he said, "and eventually what we fundamentally are becomes clear. Then body, senses, and mind are an expression of our wholeness."

The three vehicles of Self-Realization, according to Robert Adams:
- You have a deep longing or a deep feeling to be by yourself.
- You have a deep feeling or deep desire to always be in *Satsang* (to be in communion with the Self).
- You have a deep feeling or deep desire to be around people like yourself and not be around "worldly" people.   (*see* <u>Silence Speaks</u>)

Social media are a mechanism for:
- Capturing attention
- Manipulating attention
- Consuming attention

They are unlike anything else that's come along
(See "I Can Haz All Your Votes" in The Economist 11/2017

The three forefathers:
- Abraham
- Isaac
- Jacob

Towards the end of the 2015-2016 basketball season, the defending champion, Golden State Warriors, lost to a much lesser team. A couple of hours later, head coach, Steve Kerr, channeled the movie "Animal House" to jokingly call his team's performance:

- "Fat
- Drunk
- Stupid."

wrote Rusty Simmons in his sports column. He concluded by saying that "the Warriors were

- Agile
- Engaged
- Savvy

in their victory over their main rival, the San Antonio Spurs on the next night.
"San Francisco Chronicle" Sports Section" 4/4/16

Mich Jezerich interviewed Henry Giroux on KPFA radio (1/27/16). Giroux talked about the degradation of education today in America. The discussion moved to the book, <u>Pedagogy of the Oppressed,</u> by Paulo Freire, that was banned by the Tucson Arizona school district. Giroux said that the book changed the lives of thousands of educators by giving them a powerful language to carry on their struggles to do what's right for the students. He said there were three important teachings in the book:

- The nature of the educational system. It is a banking system with information poured into the heads of the kids, with no sense of agency on their part. The system is an assault on the imagination, said Giroux.
- Education is about possibility. Schools are a serious place where students are unfinished in knowing their own possibilities and realizing their own sense of agency.
- Educators must have the courage to be public intellectuals and carry the responsibility to work on the great social, ethical, and political issues of the day.

" I had three chairs in my house:
- One of them for solitude
- Two of them for friendship
- Three for society." ---Henry David Thoreau

Sherry Turkle begins her book, <u>Reclaiming Conversation</u>, subtitled <u>The Power of Talk in a Digital Age</u> with this quotation. She wrote, "these three chairs plot the points on a virtuous circle" linking
- Conversation
- Capacity for empathy
- Self-reflection

All of these are being compromised in this digital age in which people continuously relate to their devices more than to each other. Which reminds me of the New Yorker cartoon --- two people are the only ones at a funeral and one says to the other, "But he had so many friends on Facebook."

Thich Nhat Hanh explains in his book, <u>How to Sit</u>, that usually our body is doing something; we are not aware of our breath; and our mind is wandering. But as soon as we sit and pay attention, these three things:
- Body
- Mind
- Breath

come together and you become fully present in the "here and now" as we:
- Take care of our body
- Take care of our mind
- Take care of our breath.

The breath is the "harmonizer" between mind and body as it becomes regular, calm, harmonious, and brings the fruits of peace, joy, and ease.

Corroborating evidence for the existence of a real external world:
- seeing
- touching
- hearing   Chögyam Trungpa

from my own senses and from the senses of the other people around me,
thus, seeing the things of daily life as real, direct. and simple.

In <u>The Heart of the Buddha's Teaching,</u> Thich Nhat Hanh discourses on the basic Buddhist teachings of how suffering can be understood and a course of action followed that transforms suffering into:

- Peace
- Joy
- Liberation

Buddha attained enlightenment through his suffering. During the forty-five years of his teaching career, he showed how everyone else can do the same. Thich Nhat Hanh refutes the idea that Buddha taught only suffering as in the doctrine of the three forms of suffering:

- Suffering as suffering, as with a toothache.
- Suffering of composite things, as when a loved one passes.
- Suffering associated with change, as when we age.

He wrote, "Buddha taught the truth of dwelling happily in things as they are."

Thich Nhat Hanh says the practice of mindfulness allows us to:

- Recognize our negative habit energies
- Embrace our negative habit energies
- Transform our negative habit energies

They are the shadow side of the seeds of consciousness embedded in our beings.
From his book, <u>Understanding Our Mind</u>

Work is actual physical involvement with:

- Objects
- People
- Energies around that involvement

Chögyam Trungpa

The seeds of our consciousness influence the way we see and experience things:

- Perception of things-in-themselves. Thich Nhat Hanh says this is direct apprehension of reality.
- Perception as a representation. We do this when we overlay the directness of perception with the contents of our memory. We make judgements. These can be "true" or "false," depending upon our Facebook subculture; or if we're out on the moors on a foggy night, we might see and hear all sorts of things.
- Image as the experience of dreams or other psychic manifestations.
  from Understanding Our Mind

On Being Certain, Robert A. Burton's book in which he tackles the problem of how we know that we know and how we can believe that we are right even when we are wrong. He gives three concepts for understanding the workings of our brains:

- Modules (called a "mental organ" by Stephen Pinker),
- Hierarchical structures
- Emergent phenomena

He gives an example. Your retina detects an orange-and-black fluttering. Various modules in the visual cortex detect such properties as vertical motion, horizontal motion, color, shape, and size. The output from the modules is sent up the hierarchical network to emerge as the consciousness of a butterfly. Just how is still a mystery.

In his next book, A Skeptic's Guide to the Mind, Burton wrote that " our brains have evolved piecemeal:

- Contradiction
- Inconsistency
- Paradox

are built into our cognitive machinery. We are hardwired to experience unjustified feelings about ourselves, our thoughts, and our actions. We possess an irrepressible curiosity and desire to understand how the world works. We have developed an uncanny ability to see patterns whether or not they exist outside of our perceptions.

Swami Ramakrishnananda Puri, a devotee of "The Hugging Saint", Mata Amritananda Devi, wrote, in his book, <u>Amritastakam</u>, that spiritual seekers should engage in self-evaluation to compare themselves, not to the spiritual qualities of the great masters, but to themselves. We should, he writes, pay attention to three components:

- The regularity of our lapses
- How long our lapses last
- Their severity

If you have no lapses or no concern for them, that's ok too. If you're on this path, then for example, he writes that if we lose our patience-- we should ask how we lose it and how long we are out of sorts:

- Do we lose it for a few minutes?
- Do we lose it for a few hours?
- Do we lose it for a few days?

Also, we should know when we lose it:

- Are we just feeling mental agitation?
- Are we expressing ourselves out loud with words?
- Are we physically acting out?

"'*Mundus vult decipi*'—the world wants to be deceived. To live without deception presupposes standards beyond the reach of most people whose existence is largely shaped by:

- Compromise
- Evasion
- Mutual accommodation.

Could they face their

- Weakness
- Vanity
- Selfishness

without a mask?" These are words of Abraham Joshua Heschel, harvested from a Google search

Buddhadasa Bhikku discusses the Threefold Buddhist Training, based on three practical steps:

- Morality
- Concentration
- Insight

Joseph Goldstein gives the three unwholesome states of the mind in his book, <u>Mindfulness</u>, while explaining the *"Satipathana Sutta"* discourse of the Buddha. They are:

- Greed
- Hatred
- Delusion.

He refers to Buddhadasa Bhikku who describes these three tendencies as:

- "Pulling in" – lust
- "Pushing away" – anger
- "Running in circles" – delusion

Meditation taught by the Buddha sheds the light of mindfulness on the processes of feelings:

- As they arise
- As they endure
- As they fade away.

They arise from their roots, flower, and then create their fruits. The roots of the feelings have:

- Physical causes
- Physiological causes
- Psychological causes.

Thich Nhat Hanh said that most of our feelings are neutral feelings, like not having a toothache after we've had one, or in the middle of the day, having the feeling of not being tired or hungry. He said every neutral feeling when held in mindfulness, will become a pleasant feeling.

Thich Nhat Hanh pointed out that in the halo of perception there is:

- Noticing
- Naming
- Conceptualizing"

He said our perceptions are often erroneous, so he asks us to look again to see again what we perceive. "Am I sure?", He said, is a good question because then we may take a second look and check ourselves out because when we see correctly, we see better. Our perceptions, he continued are conditioned by our many afflictions: ignorance, anger, jealousy, fear, and habit energies. We can discover perceptual errors by practicing:

- Mindfulness
- Concentration
- Deep looking

He reminds us that in the "Diamond Sutra," the Buddha said, "Where there is perception, there is deception."

Jim Imhofe, an 84-year-old Republican senator from Oklahoma since 1994, was still in office in 2019. He wrote a book titled <u>The Greatest Hoax: How the Global Warming Conspiracy Threatens Your Future</u>. When asked how he keeps getting elected, he said, "It's simple:

- God
- Gays
- Guns."

"We can never
- Sneer at the stars
- Mock the dawn
- Scoff at the totality of being"

An Abraham Joshua Heschel quote fished out of Google

Hannah Arendt's insights into humans' relationship with nature and the built environment present a different analysis from Buddha's discourses on the five heaps that make up the human condition (form, feelings, perceptions, mental constructs, and consciousness). Her views were presented by Professor Peter Cannavo on philosopher C.S. Soong's radio program, "Against the Grain" (KPFA 10/7/15). Arendt sees three basic activities of humans:
- Labor: This is the way we sustain ourselves as biological creatures
- Work: This is how we create places and things from designs and plans; things that endure beyond us
- Action: This is how we create using words and deeds in the realm of collective and social reality.

This is a very Western dualistic viewpoint on the nature of human reality, in which nature is manipulated from the outside. It's not one of a being infused, embedded, and merged with reality.

Jochen Bittner wrote an opinion piece *"Who Will Win the New Great Game?"* (NYT 4/16/2018). "Call it the Game of Threes. It involves three prime players:

- Russia
- China
- The West

which are competing in three ways:

- geographically
- intellectually
- economically.

And there were three places in 2018 where the different claims to power clash: Syria, Ukraine, and the Pacific. Many of the defining conflicts of our time can be defined through combinations of these three sets."

A simple physical system, like a balloon filled with helium or, even somewhat, a bottle of water, can be modeled as an "ideal" gas composed of a chaotic frenzy of little hard atomic or molecular balls bumping into each other and off the walls. Such a system is described by three parameters:

- Pressure   **P**
- Volume   **V**
- Temperature   **T**

They are related by the Ideal Gas Law, **PV=NkT**, where the new parameters are **N**, the number of molecules and **k** the fundamental Boltzman constant of statistical mechanics. Put the values of these parameters into the formula; then you derive the number of molecules in a big bottle of beer. It is called Avogadro's number, $\mathbf{6.023 \times 10^{23}}$ which is more than a million times the number of grains of sand on all the beaches of planet Earth. This proves, without a doubt, that we humans are very very very high-level creatures. Imagine if you had so many legos made of energetic little masses. Answers to the who and why we are what we are questions lie in a more subtle realm.

Another equation, given by Shinzen Young on his website, is **S=PR** where the letters represent:

- Suffering   **S**
- Pain   **P**
- Resistance   **R**

For a given amount of pain, the more you resist, the greater is the suffering.

Charles Blow writes (5/15/2019 NYT) We are living through a flagrant display of a white male exertion of

- power,
- authority and
- privilege,

a demonstration meant to show that they will forcefully fight any momentum toward demographic displacement, no matter how inevitable the math.

Mathieu Ricard, the Buddhist monk, wrote that three problems of the current age consist of reconciling:

- The demands of the economy
- The search for happiness
- Respect for the environment

His book is <u>Altruism: The Power of Compassion to Change Yourself and the World</u>. He wrote that these imperatives correspond to:

- A short timescale
- A middle timescale
- A long timescale

On these scales are superimposed three types of interests:

- Our interests
- The interests of those close to us
- The interests of all sentient beings.

Prominent historian Yuval Harari and Nobel Prize winner, Danny Kahneman, two Israelis, discuss, on youtube.com in English, the theme "Death is an Option". Mostly, it's Kahneman listening while Harari states that the eternal 3 scourges of mankind:

- Old age
- Sickness
- Death

are coming to an end. They are no longer governed by medieval myths of a grim reaper, or evil spirits of disease, or bad karma. In scientific circles and for the rich enough, they only present technological problems as we progress into a world of class-based human species. Medicare will not cover body transplants. Some rich people will live "forever."

"The Masters of Mind Control"(4/23/2018) is a "Time Magazine" article by Hailey Sweetland Edwards. She interviewed Ramsay Brown, founder of the startup company, "Boundless Mind", formerly called "Dopamine Labs." Brown is a neuroscientist whose company's mission is to disrupt America's addiction to technology. He said that there is a three-part process:

- Trigger
- Action
- Reward.

that is the basis for the brain's habit-forming loop. T. Dalton Combs, the other principle person of "Boundless Mind", said that if you're trying to get someone to establish a new behavior -"to really glue it in tight"- computer engineers can draw on various types of feedback loops such as offering users a reward like some points or a cascade of "likes." Using variable rewards, the persuasive technology platforms have the ability to engineer "surprise and delight."

Things are organized in Buddhism. There are four noble truths, five hindrances, five aggregates or heaps, and an eightfold way. Here's another triple elucidated by Joseph Goldstein – the three distortions of experience which run counter to the first of the ways to enlightenment, Right View:

- Distortion of perception – as when a rope is mistaken for a snake
- Distortion of the mind – as when we get scared at the mistaken snake
- Distortion of view – as can be seen on Fox TV news reports by the deniers of evolution, by the deniers of climate change, and by the litany of tweets coming out of the White House in the years after 2016.

Colin McGinn proposes a three-fold taxonomy of ideas:

- Memes
- Dreams
- Themes   which is the title of his piece in "The Stone" (NYT 12/7/2015)

"Waking Up as a Meme,"a Ted Talk by András Arató, a retired Hungarian engineer known on the internet as Hide-the-Pain Harold. His image as photos taken by a professional photographer have gone viral. He smiles in the photos, but people wonder what is behind the smile. He said that he doesn't want his image to be used for three things:

- Politics
- Religion
- Sex

because these topics are too divisive. (See
https://www.youtube.com/watch?v=FScfGU7rQaM)

The Red Guard Generation and Political Activism in China, Guobin Yang's book, is discussed by Ian Johnson in his "New York Review of Books" article (10/27/16) on China's cultural revolution. Yang writes how the Party's control of information and images created a world of:

- Enchantment,
- Mesmerization
- Danger

"A world that combined a sense of possibilities and hopes with a sense of danger and threat." In a real sense, they created their own reality, like some people we know.

David Brooks decries the state of the country before the 2016 election. (NYT 10/25/16) This election has also presented members of the educated class with an awful possibility: that their pleasant social strata may rest on unstable molten layers of:

- Anger
- Bigotry
- Instability."

As every politician knows, what concerns constituents most is:

- Food
- Clothing
- Shelter.

Climate scientist, Eric Rehm, writing in *commondreams.org* (11/26/2015) was hopeful about how the Paris conference on climate change might have turned out. He gave the litany of Bill McKibben's "Do the Math," identifying three simple numbers that activists can use:

- We need to keep global warming below 2 C.
- To do that, we can only emit roughly 565 more gigatons of carbon into the atmosphere.
- Scariest of all, the amount of fossil fuel recoverable under current economic conditions is five times that, or 2,795 gigatons.

Joseph Goldstein divides the steps of the eightfold way to enlightenment into three groups:

- The Morality Steps: Right Speech, Right Action, and Right Livelihood
- The Concentration Steps: Right Effort, Right Mindfulness, and Right Concentration
- The Wisdom Steps: Right Thought and Right View.

Our prefrontal cortex (PFC) needs a rest from the assaults of contemporary capitalist culture. Robert Lustic gives three methods to get that rest

- Sleep
- Mindfulness
- Exercise

in his book, <u>The Hacking of the American Mind,</u>

Jean Klein wrote that we must see the situation and at the same time see how it echoes in us as feeling and thought. Thus, the facts of a situation must include our own reactions to it:

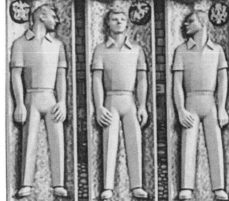

- Perceive the situation
- Free from interpretation
- Free from judgment.

Thich Nhat Hanh said of the Buddha, "He was a human being. But he had much

- Insight
- Wisdom
- Compassion

He knew how to suffer and so he suffered less."
No Mud No Lotus 2014

The rules of the science of American Slavery allowed enslavers to rape or murder their property without legal consequences. " Enslaved people could

- own nothing,
- will nothing and
- inherit nothing.

They were legally tortured, including those working for Jefferson himself." From the article by Nikole Hannah-Jones in the New York Times retrospective (8/14/2019) of the 400th anniversary of the start of slavery in America by 20 slaves bought from an English pirate who stole them from a Portuguese slaver.

S.N. Goenka, the Burmese Indian meditation master, explains the last step of the eightfold way, *samma-ditthi*, right understanding. It develops in three stages:

- Wisdom acquired by hearing or reading, which leads to belief.
- Intellectual understanding showing that the wisdom is logically sound and of some benefit.
- Wisdom experienced within one's own body-mind complex:
  - ➤ *Anicca*: Experience that everything is continuously arising, changing, and passing away
  - ➤ *Anatta*: There is no "I" and no "mine" since nothing within the physical and mental structures lasts for more than a moment
  - ➤ *Dukkha*: Suffering if one tries to possess or hold on to something. Attachment to what is ephemeral leads to suffering.
    check out Goenka at https://www.dhamma.org/en-S/about/goenka

From a twitter post by James Clear(@JamesClear 5/17/2019): Modern society is defined by an excess of opportunity. We have more information, more products, and more options than ever before. "As a result,

- curating
- filtering
- refining

are more important skills than ever before. Those who edit best will find the signal in the noise, and presumably, be the best promoters of their brand.

Early to bed and early to rise makes one

- Healthy
- Wealthy
- Wise

Goenka gave a talk at the UN in 2002, titled "Buddha, The Super Scientist for World Peace." He said that the world is afflicted by the maladies of:

- Hatred
- Anxiety
- Fear

He also said that most of the time it is blind belief and strong attachments to our own point of view that causes the negativities leading to atrocity.

In his talk at the Google headquarters (the talk's on YouTube), Thich Nhat Hanh said that three kinds of energy can be generated by the practice of mindfulness:

- Energy of mindfulness that allows us to become alive and to become present in the here and now, and to be aware that we are alive.
- Energy of concentration that takes us out of the discursive mind and that arises from mindfulness and awareness.
- Energy of insight that is generated by mindfulness and concentration.

Energy does not come from thinking. We have the insight that we are alive which is the greatest of all miracles. We breathe out to celebrate that we are alive.

Peter Godfrey-Smith's trio is stated by Daniel C. Dennett as "Evolution by natural selection is change in a population due to:

- Variation in the characteristics of members of the population,
- Which causes different rates of reproduction, and is
- Heritable."

The three levels of the human brain:
- Primal brain inherited from the reptiles.
- Emotional brain inherited from the early mammals.
- Rational brain unique to higher mammals.

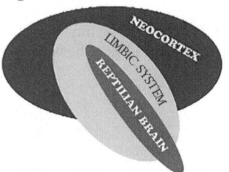

Dr. Paul MacLean, in his theory of the triune brain, says the brain has acquired three drivers, all seated up front and all of different minds! "In other words, it's as if: (His book is <u>The Triune Brain in Evolution</u>)

- An Alligator
- A gorilla
- A computer

were driving the human system!" In the course of human evolution, the brain was not transformed into a single integrated new unit. Nature superimposed each new unit upon the other so that we function with three interrelated but distinct brain systems, each with its own unique patterns and needs.

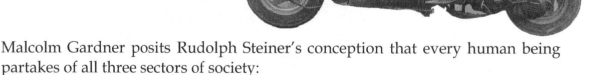

Malcolm Gardner posits Rudolph Steiner's conception that every human being partakes of all three sectors of society:
- The economic sector
- The political sector
- The cultural sector

because each person has:
- Bodily needs and capacities
- Personal rights and responsibilities
- Spiritual abilities and limitations

Gardner rejects Plato's mechanical conception of society:

- Scholars and rulers
- Guardians or soldiers
- Agriculturists and craftsman

because in Ancient Greece, human individuality was not developed as it is today in modern societies when we are not overcome as much by recurring totalitarian tendencies. Huhhh...Where's this guy been in recent centuries!

The three keys to success according to Florence Scovel Shinn:

- Rhythm
- Harmony
- Balance

The old-fashioned economy:

- Producers
- Distributors
- Consumers.

Ray Kurzweil predicted in early part of the 21st-century - One day:

- Our bodies
- Our minds
- Our machines

will all merge. His 2005 book is <u>The Singularity Is Near: When Humans Transcend Biology</u>. In 2013, he published <u>How to Create a Mind: The Secret of Human Thought Revealed</u>. At the turn of the century, his title was <u>Spiritual Machines</u>. I tried to read it then , but it was too techno-mystical for my taste. Earlier still, he wrote a great history of 20th century computing. Kurzweil's achievements are amazing. "Kurzweil Music" that produces electronic musical instruments was founded in 1982 by Stevie Wonder, Kurzweil and Bruce Cichowlas. His Kurzweil Reading Machine was the first commercial reading machine for blind people. As of 2017, he is leading a group at Google developing the "Smart Reply" feature of "Gmail" that offers 3 choices for each word typed.

It's been 15 years since I put down <u>Spiritual Machines</u>; seeing the acceleration of early 21st century technology, I now think he may be right but not correct. I fear the coming of cyborg zombies.

This is a quote from medieval poet-saint, Rumi. "Before you speak today, ask yourself these 3 questions:

- Is it true?
- Is it necessary?
- Is it kind?"

The secret of success in prayer is to be
- Simple
- Direct
- Spontaneous

according to Emmet Fox who quotes Exodus 20:25

> *And if thou wilt make me an altar of stone, thou shalt not build it of hewn*
> *stone: for if thou lift thy tool upon it, thou hast polluted it.*

Fox stated that as soon as you elaborate in prayer, you are using the intellect and the intellect cannot get spiritual contact.

see The Sermon on the Mount: The Key to Success in Life

The three-part logical syllogism consisting of:
- The major premise
- The minor premise
- The conclusion

as exemplified by the classic syllogism:
- All men are mortal
- Socrates is a man
- Therefore Socrates is mortal

Also: All men with funny hair who create chaos are clowns; Donald Trump is a man with funny hair who creates chaos; therefore...

The threefold knowledge of the Buddha according to Richard Gombrich in "Tricycle Magazine" (Fall 2012):
- Knowledge of his former births
- Knowledge of how beings are reborn according to their karmas
- Knowledge of the way to destroy the *vasanas* (the attachments to *samsara*, i.e. egoistic tendencies and hang-ups.)

Animals know how to heal themselves when they are hurt:
- They don't mate
- They don't eat
- They just rest

to let their body heal itself. These non-humans don't need
- A doctor
- A drug store
- A pharmacy

wrote Thich Nath Hahn in <u>No Mud, No Lotus.</u>

The triumvirate of tyrants in the human soul:
- "Libido Sciendi
- Libido Sentiendi
- Libido Domiendi"

Or the three universal lusts:
- Lust of the mind
- Lust of the flesh
- Lust for power

as taught to Chris Hedges at Harvard Divinity school by his professor, James Luther Adams. Hedges is the Pulitzer Prize-winning journalist, progressive author, and columnist who, in the 2010s was writing and speaking about the "Death of the Liberal Class" and the impending collapse of the American Empire.

"A bell rings to start the meditation session:
- Thoughts
- Feelings
- Perceptions

allow them all to listen to the meditation bell", says Thich Nhat Hanh

There are 72,000 *nadis* or energy channels in which consciousness and psycho-spiritual energy flow in the body according to the yogic system. Of these, three channels are the most important:
- *Ida*
- *Pingala*
- *Shushumna.*

These are the entwined caduceus snakes (medical symbol) that twist around the spine and the energy channel that runs up the center of the spine.

Vandana Shiva said that it is the mechanical mind and the mechanistic worldview that creates and nurtures the three demons:
- commodification
- greed
- scarcity   *heard on KPFA radio 2/11/2019, the Mitch Jezerich program*

Three types of New Yorkers who move to California:
- People who move to California and never look back.
- People who move to California and stay for a few months and move back east.
- People who move to California, stay there, but complain all the time: the bagels suck, the deli isn't very good, and everything closes too early at night.

The three flaws of capitalism according to Jeremy Grantham, paraphrased by Paul B. Farrell *(moneycentral.com 2012)*:
- Lack of a sense of ethics
- Absence of a conscience
- Absolute inability to process the finiteness of resources and the mathematical impossibility of maintaining rapid growth in physical output.

This last one is its greatest flaw; the "Myth of Perpetual Growth," the pseudo-scientific justification for modern capitalism's growth without "externalities." This is inimical to life on planet earth.

The three forms of late-twentieth-century information:
- Text
- Audio
- Video

But now, having passed through the digital divide into the 21st century, there is a group of biohacking "grinders" with various sensors implanted in their bodies. The Catalan dancer, Moon Ribas, has sensors implanted in her feet connected online to seismographs. She can feel just about every earthquake happening on the earth. as she does her dances. (https://www.cnn.com/style/article/moon-ribas-cyborg-smart-creativity/index.html)

The brain is a pattern sensor. It can potentially process infinite varieties of information feeds. After the singularity, however, computers will do a better job; says Ray Kurzweil.

A classic American breakfast where if you order:
- Two eggs over easy
- Toast
- Coffee

you usually also get a side of home fries and, of course, butter, jam, cream for the coffee, and ketchup for the home fries. This all would cost a dollar in Manhattan of the 1970s and is getting close to fifteen dollars in the San Francisco Bay Area in 2019. However, when I was caring for my parents in geriatric Florida in the early 2000s, I could get three breakfasts for two bucks consisting of: a basket of bagels, a basket of Danish, and two eggs over easy. toast, coffee, and home fries along with all the accouterments.

David Brooks writes (NYT 5/14/2019), "A society is healthy when its culture counterbalances its economics. When you have a capitalist economic system that emphasizes

- Competition
- Dynamism
- Individual self-interest

you need a culture that celebrates

- Cooperation
- Stability
- Committed relationships

We don't have that. We have a culture that takes the disruptive and dehumanizing aspects of capitalism and makes them worse."

Threefold nature of the human being, according to Rudolph Steiner (1861-1925):

- Neuro-sensorial
- Rhythmic
- Metabolic

which can also be expressed as:

- Head
- Heart
- Guts

This reflects onto society as:

- Education-research
- Politics-administration
- Agriculture-production

A white paper by Joseph Stiglitz is quoted by Michael Ignatieff (*New York Review of Books 7/10/14*), arguing that the fiscal crisis of the contemporary liberal state is attributable to three interrelated phenomena:

- Rising income inequality
- Money power in politics
- Systemic tax avoidance by the super-rich and the globalized corporations.

Thomas Friedman wrote (*NYT 6/17/15*) that given the incredible power new technologies give both governments and terrorists, we need a strong American Civil Liberties Union as well as a strong National Security Agency. We need to worry about:

- Big Terrorists
- Big Criminals
- Big Brother

The three elements of a sound intellect that Charles Johnson lists in his English translation of verse 7 of <u>Patanjali's Yoga Sutras</u>: *(see page 69)*

- Direct observation
- Inductive reasoning
- Trustworthy testimony

Thich Nhat Hanh, commenting on the Buddha's teachings in <u>Awakening of the Heart</u>, states that the "Three Dharma Seals:"

- Impermanence
- No-self (or selflessness)
- Nirvana, the ground of being that is the extinction of all notions such as birth and death, permanence and dissolution, coming and going, and the one and the many

are the three basic observations of Buddhism. The Buddha also told of the "Three Doors of Liberation":

- Emptiness, meaning all entities are empty of a separate independent self.
- Signlessness, the finger pointing to the moon is not the moon or the perception of a thing is not the thing. (A Vedic proclamation is *Neti Neti,* (Not This, Not This).
- Aimlessness, Thich Nhat Hanh said, "There is nothing to do, nothing to realize, no program, no agenda".

The Buddha warned his students in his discourse "Knowing the Better Way to Catch a Snake" not to misunderstand his teachings as the preaching of nihilism. The Buddha, Thich Nhat Hanh said, enjoined his disciples to be joyous, happy, and to see reality as it really is. You don't have to be a thing or have a thing that is your very own...Don't Worry!... Be Happy!

The Dalai Lama works with 3 concepts:

- Dependent arising
- Inherent existence
- Emptiness

Any object does not exist in and of itself. It is subject to the laws of cause and effect. It has an absence of "inherent existence." Any object, person, or thing arises dependently:

- Dependent on causes and conditions
- Dependent on its parts
- Dependent on thought

Emptiness is not a leg of the above triad that is imposed on objects. It is inherent in objects; the intrinsic nature of dependent arising. Emptiness is implicit in the absence of "inherent existence." In his book, <u>How to See Yourself as You Really Are,</u> the Dalai Lama explains these ideas and offers meditations The important point he makes is that the "I" is empty. There is only the universe.

In his book, <u>The Enlightened Mind</u>, Stephen Mitchell quotes the Zen Master, Kuei Shan, "Every hour of the day and night, the Zen master hears and sees ordinary sights and sounds, but nothing is distorted. He is perfectly unattached to things...because he has eliminated:

- Delusion
- Perverse views
- Bad thinking habits

An article on memory in the "New York Review of Books"(7/10/2014) by Jerome Groopman points out the intricate triple interplay of factors in the pathology of a disease:

- The inciting agent
- The genetic makeup of the individual
- The environmental factors that may shape genetic expression.

These three factors are involved in the occurrence of dementia and Alzheimer's disease, the diversity of outcomes of AIDS after infection with HIV, and the occurrence of liver failure after contraction of hepatitis C. Researchers seek cures by:

- Finding protocols to inhibit the inciting agent
- Conducting genetic studies on populations that may or may not have a proclivity for the disease
- Improving the environment with initiatives such as improving air quality or to regulating the sale of soft drinks.

"Anonymization," the process by which data is altered so that it can no longer be traced back to an individual. Data is anonymized through three primary ways

- Suppression removes some identifying values to reduce the ways the data can be identified with a particular person
- Generalization takes specific identifying values and makes them broader, such as changing specific ages
- Noise addition switches identifying values of one individual with those from another individual   New York Times Privacy Project 2019

https://mylifeiswear.com/2017/07/14/3-sheets-to-the-wind/

Three sheets to the wind

In his book, <u>Salt Sugar Fat: How the Food Giants Hooked Us</u>
Michael Moss takes on the giant food corporations for poisoning the American and the world's diet in order to enhance their profits by bringing consumers to a "bliss point" in their consumption of:

- Salt
- Sugar
- Fat

When considering pronouncements on diet, one should always keep in mind Woody Allen's profound movie, "Sleeper" in which Woody ran a health food store in Greenwich Village in the 1970s. He went into a sleep machine for 200 years. When he woke up, they fed him ice cream, cookies, bacon, and fried pork rinds. He freaked out. He told them his food theories and they told him that his theories are all wrong according to the then-recent science of their day.

Three clergymen are debating the question of when life begins:

- The priest says, "Life begins at conception."
- The pastor says, "Life begins at birth."
- The rabbi says, "Life begins when the kids move out and the dog dies."

According to Henry Giroux there is the unholy trinity of:

- Privatization
- Deregulation
- Commodification

This has led to the dysfunctional neo-liberal state, which led to the dismantling of the public sphere, and has led to vast inequalities of:

- Wealth
- Power
- Income

throughout the world, from Manhattan to Abu Dhabi to New Delhi. Check out www.henryagiroux.com

Slavoj Zizek speaks about the Hegelian Triad in a YouTube video: https://www.youtube.com/watch?v=FZzIVCBPIO0

- Rage---the people are restless and angry with the situation in the commons; this can be a chaotic rage.
- Various groups of angry people form into an organized rebellion against the established authority.
- A new power structure is established by the rebellion.

A three-four-five triangle made from a large loop of rope with twelve equally spaced knots that the ancient Egyptian surveyors pulled out to mark off the lands after the annual floods. The name for ancient Egyptian surveyors was "rope pullers."

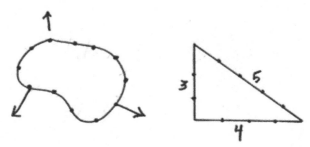

Point the short edge of the triangle to the sunrise on the day of the spring equinox. This is the east-west direction and the other short leg of the triangle points north-south. Lay out the lines, then start plowing. Make the shortest edge at least ten meters long. This method is also good for marking off the walls of a temple that the pharaoh might want to build, with the entrance facing the rising sun on the day of the spring equinox. It would probably also be good to sprinkle some drops of blood here and there, wave some incense around, chant a medley of auspicious songs, and intone prayers, and invocations.

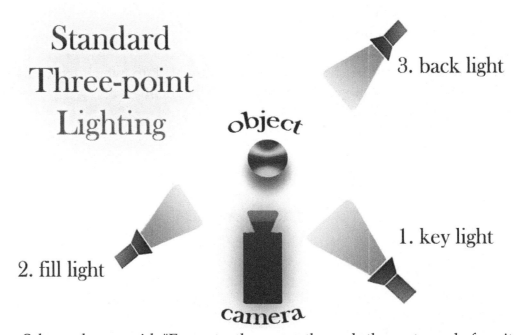

Arthur Schopenhauer said, "Every truth passes through three stages before it is recognized:
- First, it is ridiculed
- Second, it is opposed
- Third, it is regarded as self-evident."

(see the PWR Newsletter of Rossmoor, Ca 4/7/2018 edited by Paul Weisser)

A frenzy of sharks surrounded a small sinking boat in which stood, awaiting their demise:

- A priest
- A rabbi
- A lawyer

The priest jumped overboard praying, "Dear God receive my soul." Then the rabbi dove in intoning the same prayer. When the lawyer jumped in, all the sharks lined up and he was able to jump from the back of one shark to the back of another all the way to the shore to be saved. Two people were walking along the shore. One said, "Look at that. It's a miracle!" The other said, "No it's not. It's just professional courtesy."

Rub-a-dub-dub, three men in a tub, and who do you think they be?

- The butcher
- The baker
- The candlestick-maker

all put out to sea.

Three degrees of freedom of a body (e.g. an airplane) moving in 3 dimensions about its center of mass:

- Pitch (nose up-tail down to tail up-nose down)
- Roll, (or banking of wings up and down
- Yaw (with the plane zigzagging across the flight path.)

So, there's 6 degrees of freedom in all. The plane takes off, flies from New York, travels to Chicago and lands in our 3-dimensional world and along the way it is pitching, rolling, and yawing.

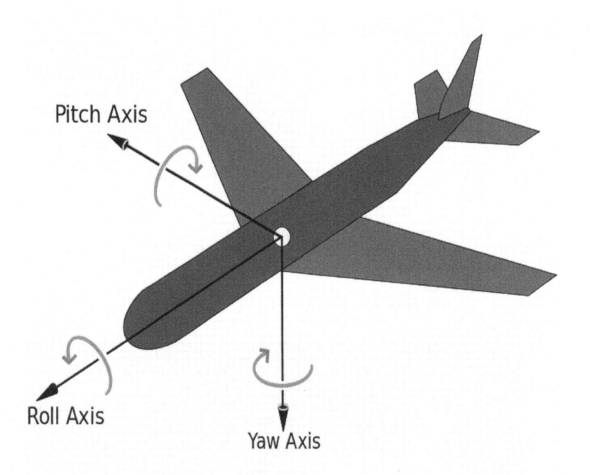

Christianity brought to ethical thought three moral ideas disruptive to the ancient world which also laid the groundwork for the flowering of Humanism a millennium later:

- Free will; the freedom of choice to do the right thing
- Christianity placed more weight on conscience, on the spirit over the letter of the law
- Idea of a common humanity, all men are brothers.

This was pointed out by the atheist philosopher, Luc Ferry, in <u>A Short History of Thought</u>.

Three kinds of men who fail to understand women:
- Young men
- Middle-aged men
- Old men *From the Old Celtic Triads*

The Sage in the "Ashtavakra Gita" tells his disciple, "You are Pure Consciousness and Bliss." He tells him that this whole universe appears like the illusion of a snake upon a rope. He tells his disciple:
- Do not fall for the illusion
- See reality as it is
- Live happily see the great commentary by Swami Chinmayananda

(It surprises me that some people don't get this. Look, you're walking along in the country and perceive a long curvy thing on the ground that your mind takes to be a snake and your mind scares you, but, when you realize that it is only a piece of rope, the fear is gone...just so with the things of our lives - this is tough to realize when things go south. And about the illusion of our common-sense world, ask any atomic physicist. Rupert Spira says this understanding of the illusion is the first step, next comes knowing the reality of the rope.

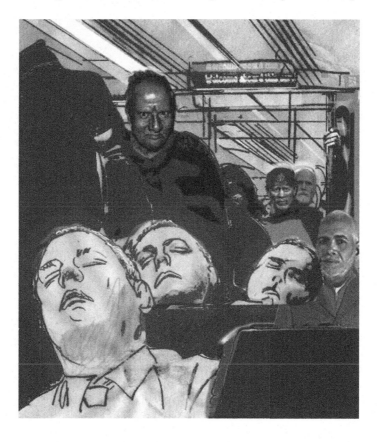

A COMPILATION OF TRIADS

http://wolf.mind.net/library/celtic/triads/triads.htm

The Traditional Laws, Customs, and Wisdoms of The Pre-Christian Celtic People of What Is Now Known as Scotland, Wales, and Ireland

Volume 1 by John F. Wright http://www.egreenway.com/druids/triadswright1995.htm

http://www.compassrose.org/folklore/irish/Irish-Proverbs/irish-triad.html

The triad originated as a simple memory device before the Irish learned to read and write. Laws, history, and lessons were often taught and memorized in this form. Here is an example.

Three things which the one having patience will gain:
- Love
- Tranquility
- Succor   *Celtic triad*

There is a web site that contains a large collection of trichotomies. See the Wikipedia entry on Trichotomy (philosophy) Here is an example:

Alan Watts' three world views:
- Life as machine (Western)
- Life as organism (Chinese)
- Life as drama (Indian).
  Wiki trichotomy

Three things lovable in a person:
- Tranquility,
- Wisdom
- Kindness   *Celtic triad*

Kant's 3 higher faculties of cognition:
- Understanding
- Judgment
- Reason *Wiki trichotomy*

There are three things to be commended in those that possess them:
- Wisdom in talk
- Justice in actions
- Excess in nothing *Celtic triad*

There are three things which the happy will gain:
- Prosperity
- Honor
- Ease of conscience. *Celtic triad*

There are three kinds of people:
- The average person who does good for good and evil for evil
- The good person, who does good for evil
- The evildoer who does evil for good.   *Celtic triad*

The three deficiencies that the people in Aldous Huxley's <u>Brave New World</u> felt:
- Nature
- Religion
- Literature.

Hegel's 3 Spirits:
- Subjective Spirit
- Objective Spirit
- Absolute Spirit.   *Wiki trichotomy*

Three things which the humble will gain:
- Plenty
- Happiness
- Love of their neighbors.   *Celtic triad*

Saint Thomas Aquinas's 3 intellectual potencies:
- Imagination
- Cogitative power (or, in animals, instinct)
- Memory (and, in humans, reminiscence)

Wiki trichotomy

Three things excellent in a person:
- Diligence
- Sincerity
- Humility
Celtic triad

Three things which come from peace:
- Increase of possessions
- Improvement of manners
- Enlargement of knowledge
Celtic triad

Karl Popper's 3 worlds:
- Physical things and processes
- Subjective human experience
- Culture and objective knowledge
Wiki trichotomy

Three ways to know a person:
- By their discourse
- By their conduct
- By their companions   *Celtic triad*

Louis Zukofsky's 3 aesthetic elements:
- Physical
- Vital
- Human   *Wiki trichotomy*

There are three falsehoods:
- Falsehood of speech
- Falsehood of silence
- Falsehood of demeanor

for each one of these will make another believe what they ought not. *Celtic triad*

Sir Francis Bacon's 3 faculties of mind:
- Memory
- Reason
- Imagination *Wiki trichotomy*

Three companions on the high road to Union with the Void:
- A patient, poor person
- A reflective, wise person
- A tolerant reformer *Celtic triad*

Harari wrote that three main factors prevent people from realizing that the order organizing their lives exists only in their imagination: (see *Sapiens*)
- "The imagined order is embedded in the material world, for example, the buildings, products in the stores, and the shape, size, and layout of their houses.
- The imagined order shapes our desires for such things as romance, vacations, fashions, movies, restaurants, and educational degrees.
- The imagined order is cultural and sub-cultural as we share many of our inner subjective experiences and understandings with others, be they a few close friends or thousands or millions of other people going to the same church, riding the same bus, or rooting for the same team."

<u>The Triple Package: How Three Unlikely Traits Explain the Rise and Fall of Cultural Groups in America</u>, by Amy Chua and Jed Rubenfeld, in which they list those traits that they believe lead some subcultural groups to be more successful than others:

- A superiority complex
- Insecurity
- Impulse control

The groups that they see meeting these criteria are Chinese, Jewish, Indian, Iranian, Lebanese, Nigerians, Cuban exiles, and Mormons. I have not read the book, but I wonder what their criteria for success is: love and compassion, income, the stability of the family, incarceration rates, or happiness. Two of the least successful groups are probably urban African Americans and indigenous people. These people, not many generations ago, lived through slavery, racial genocide, and cultural genocide, and they are still under the influences of ethnic cleansing and segregation.

Three errors not acknowledged:

- Fear of an enemy
- The torment of love
- A jealous person's evil suspicion of a mate.   *Celtic triad*

Three things that resemble each other:

- A bright sword which rusts from long staying in the scabbard.
- Bright water which stinks from long-standing.
- Wisdom which is dead from long disuse.   *Celtic triad*

C. S. Peirce's 3 universes of experience:

- Ideas
- Brute fact
- Habit   *Wiki trichotomy*

Three things each very like the other:

- An old blind horse playing the harp with his hoofs
- A pig in a silk dress
- A merciless person prating about piety   *Celtic triad*

Three things not easy to check:
- The stream of a cataract
- An arrow from a bow
- A rash tongue   *Celtic triad*

Jacques Lacan's 3 orders:
- Real
- Symbolic
- Imaginary   *Wiki trichotomy*

Three-piece suit

Three things that stay longest in a family:
- Fighting
- Drinking
- Red hair   *Celtic triad*

Three things which are not hidden:
- A straw in a shoe
- An awl in a bag
- A harlot in a crowd   *Celtic triad*

Three techniques for controlling the conversation or interview so that you are sure to get your main points across:
- Bridge: Move from an area in the conversation that you don't want to discuss and get the conversation back to your message. For example, if the interviewer asks, "What do you think of BIP?" then you answer, "It's really important that we first consider BAP"
- Hook: Get the interviewer to follow-up on your first point allowing you to get a second point in by saying, "There are two very important considerations that must be taken into account before we support the BIP proposal"
- Flag: Emphasize the key point or points you want the audience to remember by simply giving them a verbal clue about what is important such as saying, the most important thing to remember is . . . "BAP" or "If you remember nothing else, please remember these two points.

See the Advocacy Action Plan by the American Library Association

Jobs at the bottom of the industrial pyramid most likely to be taken by robots because they are:
- Dull
- Dangerous
- Dirty.   "The Economist" magazine of March 2014

Wikipedia, in its entry on hendiatris, states that the Japanese said a similar thing about jobs at the "bottom" during their boom years. Illegal immigrants performed the work that was Kiken, Kitsui, and Kitanai, or:

- Dangerous
- Difficult
- Dirty.

The elements of a Hollywood drama:

- Villains
- Victims
- Heroes

There are three things, and any who move them are accursed:

- The boundary of land
- The course of water
- The sign of a road or track.   *Celtic triad*

Three keys that unlock the secrets of the soul:

- Heavy drinking
- Violent temper
- Innocent trust.   *Celtic triad*

In "Hive Mentalities"("New York Review of Books" (12/20/2018), Tim Flannery lists three social insects:

- bees
- ants
- termites

He reviews Buzz The Nature and Necessity of Bees by Thor Hanson and Underbug: An Obsessive Tale of Termites and Technolgy by Lisa Margonelli. The first book documents the current apocalyptic problems of the bees. The second book tells about how robotic researchers, thinking that termites were robotic, found them to be quite individualistic.

The three sweetest sounds:

- Sound of the quern*,
- Lowing of the cow
- Cry of a child.   *Celtic triad*
    * *(a quern is a primitive hand-operated mill for grinding grain.)*

"The World is Fast," an article (NYT 11/5/2014) by Thomas L. Friedman's in which he writes, that "because of the three biggest forces on the planet:
- Globalization making workers, investors and markets much more interdependent
- Mother Nature-global warming
- Moore's Law – the digital revolution"

Three things that a man should never be without:
- A cat
- A chimney
- A woman of the house   *Celtic triad*

Three clouds that obscure the sight of wisdom:
- Forgetfulness
- Ignorance
- Little knowledge   *Celtic triad*

There are three things in life that you should never do ambivalently:
- Get married
- Buy a house
- Go to war

written in the New York Times by Thomas L. Friedman as Obama prepared to go to war in Iraq. *(9/14/14)*

Three sources of new life:
- A woman's stomach
- A hen's egg
- A wrong forgiven   *Celtic triad*

Three things in the world between which there is a wonderful difference:
- The faces of people
- The utterances of people
- The writings of people   *Celtic triad*

Three things that run swiftest:
- A stream of fire
- A stream of water
- A stream of falsehood   *Celtic triad*

It is highly questionable wrote Harari, that the Europeans could have conquered the world without: *Sapiens*
- The practical knowledge
- Ideological justification
- Technological gadgets provided to the imperial project by science that needed the support of empire and the investments of the capitalists for its progress

In a very far out book, <u>Deep Space</u>, Govert Schilling points out that we live in the "Local Group" consisting of 59 galaxies, most of which are dwarf galaxies. The "Local Group" contains three large spiral galaxies:
- Andromeda Galaxy contains one trillion stars in a region 200,000 light-years wide that is 2.5 million light years from Earth
- Milky Way contains between 200 to 400 billion stars in a region of space 100,000 to 180,000 light-years wide
- Triangulum Galaxy contains 40 billion stars in a region 2,000 to 3,000 light-years wide that is 60,000 light years from earth.

Most of the remaining dwarf galaxies in the "Local Group" are arrayed as satellites of these three large spiral galaxies. Our Local group itself is a part of the larger "Laniakea Supercluster." Wikipedia states that Laniakea was not defined until 2014. This super-cluster encompasses 100,000 galaxies stretched out over 160,520 million light-years and it has a mass of one hundred thousand trillion suns which is about a hundred thousand times the mass of our Milky Way Galaxy. Superclusters are spread, in turn, throughout the universe in a sort of soap sudsy array of matter and energy composed of void spaces encompassed by bubbles of matter and energy, 95% of which is dark and only inferred to exist but not "seen" by human senses or their technological extensions.

Dmitri Mendeleev published a periodic table of elements in 1869 that eventually developed into the one used today with 92 naturally occurring elements. Mendeleev left spaces in his table for elements that had not yet been discovered in his day, but that he thought would be found in the future. All the gaps he left have been filled in and new extraordinary man-made elements have been discovered with slots for them appended to the table. Will they ever get far out enough to discover the element, JohnColtranium?

A century later, physicists developed a lower order table called "The Standard Model of Elementary Particles". It is lower order because the biggest of the elementary particles, the proton, is a hundred thousand times smaller than the smallest atom in the chemical periodic table we all saw in our science classrooms. The physicists left an open slot in their table in the late 1960s that wasn't filled in until experiments at the Cern Hadron Supercollider allowed them to discover the missing piece called the Higgs boson in 2013!

The most important of the elementary particles are the
- Electron
- Proton
- Neutron

discovered in the years 1897, 1922, and 1932 respectively. Since then, a confusing collection of other particles has been discovered and they have been placed into their appointed slots within the Standard Model's pigeonholes. Most of these particles exist for only very, very short periods of time before they decay into other particles. The electron lives "forever," a free neutron has a lifetime of 886 seconds, and the proton lives for a time longer than the age of the universe.

There is a profusion of "threeness" in the world of elementary particles. The proton and neutron are, it turns out, not elementary particles! They are composed of **3** quarks each. The quarks come in a pair called UP and DOWN. Their electrical charges come in factional thirds: +2/3 for the UP quark and -1/3 for the DOWN quark. The proton is made of 2 UP quarks and 1 DOWN quark, so the proton's electrical charge is **2/3 + 2/3 – 1/3=3/3 =1**. The neutron is composed of 1 UP and 2 DOWN quarks giving it an electrical charge of **2/3 - 1/3 - 1/3 = 0.**

Quarks also come in colors: red, green, and blue...not "seeing" colors, but metaphorical colors for "threeness." All three quarks in each proton and in each neutron are colored in such a way that they combine to be "white." Thus, there are 3 UP quarks: red-up, blue-up, and green-up and a similar triple of down quarks.

Another particle, the gluon mediates the forces between the quarks. Here's a metaphor. Two ice skaters on a slick frozen lake throw a heavy ball back and forth between them. As they do, they slide apart and so the ball mediates the force that causes them to repel one another. This ball is a metaphor stretched beyond the breaking point to "explain" the gluon's mediation of the strong force because the further apart the quarks become, the stronger is the force that attracts them. Weird, huh? That's why the proton system is so stable and why the particles mediating the force are called gluons. They come in colors too!

There's still more "threeness". The electron belongs to an existing triplet of siblings. Its mates are called the muon and the tau. The up-down quark pair is also in a triplet of pairs along with the "top-bottom" pair and the" charmed-strange" pair. In both cases the extra siblings are heavier and have shorter lifetimes.

There is a great video on YouTube by Richard Feynman on the 2-slit experiment in which he discusses the essential basics of quantum mechanics and ends his lecture discussing the preconditions for science:
- The ability to do experiments,
- Honesty in reporting the results, and
- Minds to interpret the results that are not biased as to the way nature should behave.

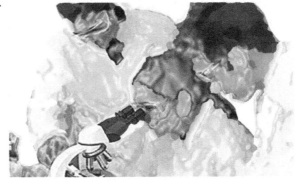

The three wise men cocktail:
- 1 part Scotch (e.g. Johnnie Walker)
- 1 part Tennessee whiskey (e.g. Jack Daniels)
- 1 part Kentucky Bourbon (e.g. Jim Beam)

What is science about? Pedro Domingos wrote in The Master Algorithm that it is:
- Prediction
- Explanation
- Understanding.

Ultimately, if your models don't make accurate predictions on new data, you can't be sure you've understood or explained the underlying phenomena."

The heresy of Michael Faraday, according to early 19th-century science, was that he questioned the existence of magnetic poles. He had three reasons:

- Why should arbitrary points or "poles" at the ends of magnets act as centers of forces?
- Nobody had ever observed a single isolated pole
- The magnetic force field lines of a cylindrical wire coil forming an electromagnet run in circles as do a bar magnet's field lines, they do not end on "poles."   See <u>Faraday, Maxwell, and the Electromagnetic field</u> by Nancy Forbes and Basil Mahon.

Forbes and Mahon tell about Faraday's reaction to the negative feedback he received after debunking claims of some of the popular "spiritualists" of his day. "Table Turning" was popular in fashionable London of the day. Table-turners sat a group of people around a table with their hands resting on its top. Then, mystically, the table began to turn to and fro. Faraday turned the tables on the table-turners. In his letter to the "*Athenaeum*" magazine, he wrote, "What a weak, credulous, unbelieving, superstitious, bold, frightened, what a ridiculous world ours is, as far as concerns the minds of men. How full of:

- Inconsistencies
- Contradictions
- Absurdities"

"Time sits at the center of the tangle of problems raised by the intersection of:
- Gravity
- Quantum mechanics
- Thermodynamics"

This statement appears in the sixth lesson called "Probability, Time, and the Heat of Black Holes" in the book, <u>Seven Brief Lessons on Physics</u> (2014) by Carlo Rovelli. Rovelli gets on down and dishes out fundamental ideas, like a hot gravitational field, or time as an event, or an event as time, or the graininess of space and time. Rovelli showed the great progress made in physics and he lets us know about the WTF status of ideas at the current boundary of physics. He said that a threefold tangle appears in the phenomenon of Hawking's theory of heat emitted by black holes. Rovelli said the heat of black holes is like the Rosetta stone of physics written in the three languages of gravity, quantum mechanics, and thermodynamics and still awaits decipherment.

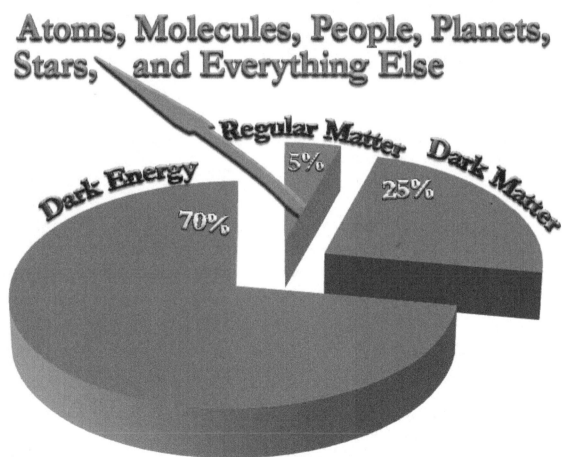

Atoms, Molecules, People, Planets, Stars, and Everything Else

Regular Matter 5%

Dark Matter 25%

Dark Energy 70%

The universe as we know it in 2019, approximately

Great stuff on youtube.com:
https://www.youtube.com/watch?v=DP8r9i9PYpo&t=5337s

"The Mind and Life XXVI Conference" from Drepung Monastery in Mundgod, Karnataka, India, was held on January 17-22, 2013. Twenty world scientists and philosophers met with His Holiness the Dalai Lama and other senior Tibetan scholars. There were about fifty people in the room. The Dali Lama sat at one end of a conference table with his interpreter. He began the conference by welcoming everyone in perfect English. He said that he preferred to hear the ideas put forth at the conference in Tibetan because his English was not good enough for highly technical matters. The ten or so principle scientists sat around the table. Some topics covered ranged from the historical sweep of science and the revolutions in our understanding of our physical universe to the nature of the mind. Scientific and the classical Buddhist philosophical methods of inquiry were studied, as well as selected topics in quantum physics, neuroscience, and Buddhist and contemporary Western views of consciousness Applications of contemplative practices in clinical and educational settings were explored. In the afternoon session of the fifth day, Lobsang Tenzin Negi, Senior Lecturer at Emory University spoke about "cognitively-based compassion training" (CBCT) which is based on teachings of the Dalai Lama's program of secular ethics. He said that one of the goals of CBCT is to bring a person to compassion for all people they may encounter, whether they be:

- Friend
- Stranger
- Enemy

It was also reported, at the conference, that in the industrialized countries of the world, there was an epidemic of:

- Isolation
- Depression
- Loneliness

Maurice Merleau-Ponty's 3 categories:

- Quantity
- Order
- Meaning   *Wiki trichotomy*

The three best friends and the three worst enemies:
- Fire
- Wind
- Water   *Celtic triad*

Three qualities which show wisdom:
- Suffering discreetly
- Forgiving injury
- Seeking knowledge   *Celtic triad*

Twenty amino acids are the building blocks that form the innumerable protein molecules making up living organisms. The double-stranded DNA molecule contains the codes for the assembly of these 20 amino acids into an organism's various larger proteins. It may take thousands of amino acids strung together by DNA mechanisms to make up a protein. Four nucleotides form the ribs of the DNA double spiral and the basis of the DNA code. The code is written in 4 different letters: A, G, C, and T which stand for these 4 nucleotide molecules: Adenine ($C_5H_5N_5$), Guanine ($C_5H_5N_5O$), Cytosine ($C_4H_5N_3O$), and Thymine ($C_5H_6N_2O_2$). How can a 4-letter alphabet be used to make a code for 20 different amino acids? Two letter codes of letter pairs such as AA, AG, AC, AT, or ... GT...TT... gives only 4X4=16 possibilities, not enough. Thus

The words of DNA, called CODONS, contain 3 letters each

These are more than enough (4X4X4=64 possible words) to code for the 20 amino acids forming the proteins of life. There can be multiple codons for each amino acid. The codons for isoleucine ($C_6H_{13}NO_2$) are ATT, ATC, ATA. There is only one codon for Methionine ($C_5H_{11}NO_2S$), ATG. There are 6 codons for Serine($C_3H_7NO_3$): TCT, TCC, TCA, TCG, AGT, AGC. And so on for the other 13 or 14 amino acids of which our cellular proteins are composed.

Three feasts due to everyone:
- The feast of baptism
- The feast of marriage
- The feast of death   *Celtic triad*

Three things that are always cold:
- A dog's nose   *Celtic triad*
- A man's elbow
- A maid's knee

Three things hard to catch:
- A stag on the mountain
- A fox in the wood
- The coin of the miserly scrooge   *Celtic triad*

Plato's model of the soul consists of three aspects:
- The rational
- The spirit
- The desires   Wiki trichotomy

The principle discoverers of the of the binary spiral structure of the DNA molecule:
- Francis Harry Compton Crick   won a Nobel Prize
- Rosaland Franklin   did not win a Nobel Prize
- James Dewey Watson   won a Nobel Prize

Linus Pauling, two-time winner of the Nobel Prize, was also searching for the DNA structure at the same time. Pauling had a career's worth of moss accumulated because knew that spheres would radiate as triple spirals. The newcomers were rolling into new territory and had no moss accumulated.

Robert Adams taught the end result of one's spiritual realization manifests as:
- Love
- Compassion
- Humility

Sarah Lazare, a staff writer for Commondreams.org, wrote a piece on American charter schools (4/27/15) called:
- "Waste,
- Fraud, and
- Lies"

Three properties of the Holy Spirit according to St. Paul:
- Creating
- Renewing
- Sanctifying

The Triangle Shirtwaist Factory fire in New York City on March 25, 1911, was the deadliest industrial disaster in the history of the city. Over 100 people died. The sound of so many bodies thudding to the cement from on high was not heard in the city again for almost 100 years. This led to the passing of labor safety laws in the United States and the eventual exportation of jobs to low wage countries without such laws --- this sentence, in the passive voice, obscures the compassionate people who passed the laws and the greedy people who exported the jobs.

The simple nuclear family:
- Mother
- Father
- Child

"Queer as a three-dollar bill." (The original bill showed a picture of Liberace, the entertainer who wore flamboyant costumes in mid-20th century America)

John Hussman, in his financial blog, wrote that patience is the most valuable trait of the endgame player, where the most common errors, (besides those resulting from ignorance of theory), are caused by one or all of the following:

- Impatience
- Complacency
- Exhaustion

The slogan of the French Revolution:

- *Liberté*   Liberty
- *Eqalité*   Equality
- *Fraternité*   Fraternity

Nicholas Kristof reviewed Fareed Zakaria's book, <u>In Defense of a Liberal Education</u> in the "New York Times" (4/16/2015) and gave Zakaria's three reasons to study the liberal arts:

- Liberal arts equip students with communications and interpersonal skills that are valuable and rewarded in a 21st-century professional life.
- We need people conversant with the humanities to help reach wise public policy decisions, even about the sciences.
- Wherever our careers lie, much of our happiness depends upon our interactions with those around us, and there's some evidence that literature nurtures a richer emotional intelligence.

The unholy trinity of world capitalism as stated by Richard Peet, talking with C.S. Song, on progressive radio station KPFA, in 2012:
- IMF
- WTO
- World Bank

From the Buddhist scriptures:
"Three cut reeds can stand only by leaning on one other"
Thich Nhat Hanh, The Heart of the Buddha's Teaching
Similarly, a table needs at least three legs upon which to stand.

In the realm of geometry and physics, triangles are the only energetically stable polygons. Do an experiment. Use cut strips of cardboard with holes punched near their ends and use those brass fasteners that spread apart and then make a triangle and a square. The three sides of the triangle balance each other as a stabile configuration, but the four sides of a square collapse into flatter and flatter diamond shapes and thus do not form a stable structure. -

Do another experiment. Use toothpicks and mini marshmallows to make a triangle and a square to see the stability of one geometry and the flimsiness of the other or use wooden barbeque skewers and regular sized marshmallows to see a larger, similar, result. Bucky Fuller talked about this and why you see all those triangles forming his geodesic domes. The ancient Greeks and the Tibetans didn't understand the energetics. Their symbol for the element of fire was the tetrahedron formed of 4 triangular faces; it's like an Egyptian pyramid with a triangular base. They were hypnotized in a Platonic realm. They saw the sharp corners of triangles "burning up" structures when tetrahedral sand particles barrel-down in the howling wind against the rocks. (For further experimentation note that 4 marshmallows and 6 toothpicks make a tetrahedron, the elemental 3D structure.)

Threeness in the corner of a cube

"Real Life on the Path of Mindfulness" is the subtitle of Chögyam Trungpa's book,

- Work
- Sex
- Money.

He writes that disciplines recommended by the great masters should be considered as training for interaction with the real-world energies of work, sex, and money. Spirituality, he writes, is about how to handle the situations of daily life.

Three pairs that never agree:

- Two married women in the same house
- Two cats with one mouse
- Two bachelors courting the same woman   *Celtic triad*

The pathological mutation of capitalism that is being spread by the "happy conspiracy" of:

- Wall Street
- Washington
- Corporate America   written *by Paul Farrell in his blog on marketwatch.com (8/29/2009*

Barack Obama's political triangulation of:
- Reality
- Public opinion
- Money

Three things every chieftain needs:
- Justice
- Peace
- An army   *Celtic triad*

"Listen to the conversations at a social gathering," Eric Butterworth said, "and you can measure the strength of the minds:
- Great minds talk about ideas
- Average minds talk about events
- Small minds talk about people"

Mahalia Jackson sings," My God is real!", with all her
- Body
- Heart
- Soul

Three qualities that we have in our meditation and daily lives that we can nurture, cultivate, and bring out:
- Precision
- Gentleness
- The ability to let go

These are given by Prema Chodron in her dharma talks in her book, <u>The Wisdom of No Escape.</u>

The threefold Buddhist training:
- Training in concentration – *samadhi*
- Training in Understanding – *panna* or *prajna*
- Training in ethical moral discipline – *sila*

When it comes to knowing that we know, Robert A. Burton gives the temporal sequence:

- Thought
- Assessment of the thought
- A feeling of correctness or knowing that we know

It's a downright mystical experience if we get the feeling of knowing before we get the thought and an AHHAA!!! moment when we get the thought and assessment simultaneously with the feeling of correctness.

Op-Ed columnist Nicholas Kristof wrote a piece in the "New York Times," "The Best News You Don't Know" (9/22/2016) that begins with some somber triples: "The world is a mess, with billions of people locked in inescapable cycles of:

- War
- Famine
- Poverty

with more children than ever perishing from:

- Hunger
- Disease
- Violence.

That's about the only thing Americans agree on. Several polls have found that about 9 out of 10 Americans believe that global poverty has worsened or stayed the same over the last 20 years." Fortunately, the one point Americans agree on is dead wrong." He goes on to report, that despite all the horrible things going on in the world, that world extreme poverty is declining, and literacy and health are improving.

Three minimal features possessed by simple organisms to allow genetic transfer to the next generation:
- Sensing the internal and external environments
- A response policy to these sensations
- Movement:

This is from Antonio Damasio's book, <u>The Feeling of What Happens " Body and Emotion in the Making of Consciousness"</u>

Damasio also pointed out the three different brains that evolution has brought to us:
- A brain that produces behavior but does not appear to have mind or consciousness, as in the nervous system of the marine snail, *Aplysia Californica*
- A brain like the human brain that produces a whole range of phenomena: behavior, mind, and consciousness
- An insect-like brain that produces behavior, likely produces a mind, and questionably produces anything like consciousness.

Native Bird Connections of Martinez, California presents education programs under the guiding principles of:
- Respect
- Reverence
- Responsibility

for the Natural World.

Brains endeavor to improve the business of:
- Sensing
- Deciding
- Moving

thereby maximizing biological value", wrote Damasio.

He also posits three selves:
- The proto-self, where the body and mind interact and bond giving rise to "proto-feelings."
- The core self, which is about the relationship between the organism and objects
- The autobiographical self that apprehends the past as well as anticipates the future. In its higher reaches, this self constitutes a "social me" as well as a "spiritual me."

The sage, Dattatreya, points out in the <u>Avadhuta Gita</u>, an ancient scripture, that three sins are committed by the enlightened one when:

- He makes pilgrimage and thereby destroys the all-pervasiveness of the Divine
- He meditates, as he destroys the Divine's transcendence of the mind
- He sings praises of the Lord thereby destroying the Divine's transcendence of speech.

Dattatreya asks the Divine to ever forgive him for these three sins.

The Babylonian Talmud talks about the three things in which the mind of a man is revealed:

- In his wine goblet
- In his purse
- In his wrath

The "triple evils" noted by Dr. Martin Luther King:

- Racism
- Economic exploitation
- Militarism

Three 19th century methods for studying localized brain function (See Michael Gazzaniga's book, Who's in Charge):

- Surgically destroy certain areas and see what happens.
- Stimulate parts of the brain electrically and see what happens.
- Study neurological patients clinically and then do autopsies after they die.

Kant's 3 categories of quantity:

- Unity
- Plurality
- Totality   Wiki trichotomy

Amos Oz and his daughter, Fania Oz-Salzberger, give a great quote at the beginning of their book, Jews and Words, about God-- He created this universe by three Sepharim:

- Number
- Writing
- Speech

These Sepharim are three of the ten emanations or angels of God contemplated in the Kaballah Wisdom Tradition.

Three ways in which mood-altering drugs can produce their magic:
- Interference with the transmission of signals from the body to the brain
- Creation of a particular pattern in the part of the brain that maps the body
- Change in the state of the body.
  (wrote Antonio Damasio in <u>Looking for Spinoza</u>)

What will happen when humanity discovers beings from a distant alien civilization? According to Paul Saffo in his 2009 edge.org piece:
- A third will want to conquer them
- A third will want to convert them
- A third will want to sell them something

Yuval Harari said that about 1000 BC, three potential orders developed, whose members could imagine all human beings governed by a single set of laws set up by these orders: *see, <u>Sapiens</u>*
- Economic order using money
- Political order of the empire
- Order of a universal religion

These orders were promulgated by:
- Merchant
- Emperor
- Prophet

During the last 3000 years, attempts made by these agents have become more and more successful.

Damasio is great at thinking in triples. He discusses Spinoza's recommendation for living "a life well-lived" - that one should come into some clarity about the big questions like: Where we are coming from?, Where we are going?, and What purpose greater than our immediate existence life could possibly have? Damasio points out that people today would be puzzled by such an injunction, by such fretting and fussing – for the only things you really need in this modern world are:

- Youth
- Health
- Good fortune

Ray Kurzweil said computation consists of three elements:
- Communication (between computers & between the parts of a computer)
- Memory
- Logic gates (a pattern of bits comes into the gate and is transformed before coming out in a new pattern)

B.R. Ambedkar's exhortation to the lower castes of India:
- Educate
- Agitate
- Organize.

He came from a low caste family and was the chief architect of the constitution of India.

The thirteenth-century Zen monk, Dogen, said, "The triple world is mind alone."
Brad Warner explicates by giving these meanings for "triple world":

- The world of thinking, feeling, and action
- The world of volition, matter, and non-matter
- The well-known: past present, and future

See Warner's web site, *http://hardcorezen.info/what-kind-of-guy-was-dogen/4383*

The Marx Brothers were a comedy team in the mid-20th century. Chico, Harpo, and Groucho were the three eldest and most prominent of the five brothers. The other two were Gummo and Zeppo. Wikipedia says five of the Marx Brothers' thirteen feature films were selected by the American Film Institute (AFI) as among the top 100 comedy films, with two of them "Duck Soup" and "A Night at the Opera" in the top twelve.

The three most powerful pistons of capitalism's growth machine:

- Capital markets
- Innovation
- The knowledge economy

See Schumpeter's column in the September 29th, 2012 issue of the "Economist."

Bobby Colomby is the leader of the popular band:

Blood, Sweat, and Tears

"We're often asked," he said, 'Does the band have any original members?' He replies, "When you're at a Yankee game you're not going to see Babe Ruth and Lou Gehrig. They're not going to be there. But what you will see is a brand, the pinstripes, and they'll be able to hit, score runs and play great defense. Because management's obligation is to recruit the best players available and put the most cohesive combination of players on the field to represent the Yankee brand. So that when the Yankees win, and they've played magnificently, no one's going to ask, "Where's the Bambino, Where's Mickey Mantle?"

There are three beauties of a land:
- the granary
- the smithy
- the school   *Celtic triad*

Three delusions prevalent in the mentalities of the super-rich as the American reported by Paul Farrell in his blog on "marketwatch.com:"
- Perpetual economic growth is possible on a planet of limited resources
- Dream New technologies will replace disappearing resources mutates into a global nightmare.
- Mutant capitalists do not need to share the future as the income gap grows and more and more people in the exploding populations are left without adequate food, water, and education.

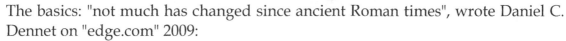

The basics: "not much has changed since ancient Roman times", wrote Daniel C. Dennet on "edge.com" 2009:
- Procreating
- Eating
- Staying alive.

I.F. Stone posits three reasons that Socrates paradoxically claimed that virtue and knowledge could not be taught and denied that he was a teacher:

- Philosophical reason – Socrates was forever searching for and not finding absolute definitions of virtue and knowledge
- Political reason – linked to his anti-democratic doctrine that one who knows should rule and the rest obey (an analogy to hiring the plumber to fix the pipes)
- Personal reason – His two most famous students, Critias and Alcibiades were horrible tyrants during their political careers when the Athenian democracy was overthrown.

I.F. Stone…The Trial of Socrates

Stone believed that there were three "political earthquakes" occurring in less than a decade that shook the Athenians' sense of internal security and led to the trial of Socrates in 399 B.C:

- The overthrow of the democracy by the Group of 400 Tyrants in 411 B.C.
- The overthrow of the democracy by the Group of 30 Tyrants in 404 B.C.
- The attempted overthrow of the democracy in 401 B.C.

Each of these totalitarian upheavals was greatly influenced by the students of Socrates.

Three philosophers were sleeping under a tree. A fourth philosopher wanting to test their philosophical skill came up and painted white dots on each of their foreheads. Then he woke them up and said, "To test your philosophical acumen, I have either painted or not painted a white dot on each of your foreheads. Look at your fellow philosophers and if you see a white dot on one or another of their foreheads, raise your hand." They looked and all three immediately raised their hands. The fourth philosopher then asked, "Who can tell if they have a white dot on their forehead and prove it?" The three looked at each other for a few hesitant longish moments and then one of them quickly said, "I have a dot. Here's the proof. Suppose I did not have a dot, then my two colleagues would immediately know that they each had a dot because they would see each other's dot and raised hand and know that the other's hand was raised because of their dot and not because of a dot on my forehead; but they hesitate-- they do not know for whose dot the other's hand is raised. This hesitation proves that my supposition is false and thus I have a dot. QED

Three forms of wisdom in Western culture, according to Alan Watts:

- Religion
- Philosophy
- Science

"Ought implies can" is an ethical formula ascribed to Immanuel Kant that claims that an agent, if morally obliged to perform a certain action, must logically be able to perform it." This sentence appears in a Wikipedia article titled "Ought implies can" found in a Google search This dyad is enlarged by Vlad Chituc and Paul Henne in their article, "The Data Against Kant"("NYT 2/21/16"), when they report on philosophical experiments with non-philosophers who considered the following triad to be important:

- Ought
- Can
- Blame

An example they give is the scenario in which two friends were applying for the same job. The first friend had the interview already and now, as he ought to do, was driving the second friend to the airport so that she could go to her interview. The car broke down on the way to the airport so the first friend could not do what he ought to have done and he was not to blame. But if the first friend sabotaged his car so that he could not do what he ought to have done, then he would be to blame.

Aristotle described three basic techniques for persuading your audience:
- Ethos - based upon your credibility
- Pathos - appeal to emotions
- Logos - persuasion by logic

Put out on the internet by Natalie Smith of Demand Media.

Susan Engel, author of <u>The Hungry Mind: The Origins of Curiosity in Childhood</u> was being interviewed on KPFA radio (3/2017). She said that the places in the school environment that evoked the most curiosity are:
- Messy
- Dynamic
- Unpredictable

She gave examples of fish tanks, terrariums, free time with other kids, and outside play in nature as the antidote for the calcification by:
- Test-taking
- Compliance with rules
- Rote learning

An American Sunday afternoon in autumn:
- Beer
- Junk food
- Football game on TV

Bruce Feiler's book, <u>Abraham</u>, is about the author's search for the heart of three faiths. On the way to Hebron and the tomb of the patriarchs, his cab driver, Nasser, said that "in Islam, you have no control over three things:
- Your money
- Your marriage
- Your death"

The three Abrahamic faiths that Bruce Feiler studies:
- Judaism
- Christianity
- Islam

They all worship the same monotheistic God, but their believers have been killing each other for millennia. God made a covenant with Abraham, who became the founding patriarch of each religion. The Jews believe that they are the specially chosen people. The Christians believe that Jesus was the one and only son of God. The Muslims believe their prophet, Mohammed, was the last and greatest messenger of God. They should check their beliefs at the swinging door of the saloon, share drinks, spittoons, cigars, dancing girls, and experience the Great Mystery beyond all beliefs, concepts, and words, for as the Hindus say, "All rivers lead to the same ocean." That is not to say that Hindus aren't capable of dastardly deeds along with all their other fellow religious brothers and sisters; especially in post-Gandhian BJP-RSS India.

Antonio Damasio asks three of the most vexing questions in his book, <u>Descartes' Error</u>. "How is it
- that we are conscious of the world around us?
- that we know what we know?
- that we know that we know?"

214

Ronald Wright begins his book, <u>A Short History of Progress,</u> with a chapter called "Gaugin's Questions":

- *"D'Ou` Venons Nous"* -Where do we come from?
- *Que Sommes Nous?* - What are we?
- *Ou` Allons Nous?* - Where are we going?

The eternal money spinners were there in ancient Sumeria. Ronald Wright wrote that the Sumerian priests were the world's first racketeers as they ran:

- Protection
- Booze
- Girls

Wright discusses Joseph Tainter's three aspects of the decay of civilization:

- The Runaway Train as seen in population increase, accelerating pollution, and the excessive concentration of wealth and power.
- The Dinosaur exemplified in the hostility to change by vested interests and inertia in all social levels.
- The House of Cards in cases where civilizations collapse very quickly not long after attaining their zenith.

"Once we are able to understand our suffering", wrote Thich Nhat Hanh in <u>No Mud No Lotus</u>, "we can transform our suffering into:
- Understanding
- Compassion
- Joy"

The crew members of the Apollo 11 Lunar Landing on July 20, 1969 were:
- Neil Armstrong, Commander
- Michael Collins, Command Module Pilot
- Edwin E. Aldrin Jr., Lunar Module Pilot

They appear in the above order, left to right in the drawing above. Collins remained in the command-service module orbiting the moon while Armstrong and Aldrin rode the lunar module down to the moon's surface. They remained there for 21 hours and 36 minutes. Upon landing on the lunar surface, Armstrong said, "One small step for man and one giant step for mankind", forgetting the letter "a" before the word "man." No matter, he is still a hero.

Benjamin Franklin once wrote: "
- Tell me and I forget
- Teach me and I remember
- Involve me and I learn

Libraries have a triple role for our society wrote Alberto Manguel in his op-ed piece (NYT 10/23/15):

- Preservers of the memory of our society
- Providers of the tools for navigating their materials
- Symbols of our identity.

Libraries are resilient, he said, and intent on surviving in an age where intellectual acts have lost prestige. He ended by noting that one of the libraries of ancient Egypt carried above its entrance the inscription: "Clinic of the Soul."

Three women on Team USA achieved a sweep of the medal podium when they won the finals of the 100-meter hurdles held in the Rio Olympics on August 18, 2016. Photographs in the Getty archives after the race show them in well-earned wonderous states of joy, bliss, and ecstasy. It would be nice if we could all share a little of their state with each and every breath we take

- Brianna Rollins took the gold medal.
- Nia Ali earned silver medal.
- Kristi Castlin won the bronze medal.

The big bad wolf and the three little pigs imprinted 20th century childhoods.

- The first little pig built a house made of straw.
- A second little pig built a house made of sticks.
- The third little pig built a house made of bricks.

The big bad wolf huffed and puffed and blew the first two houses down, but thanks to a small military budget, wise spending on infrastructure, and the reining in of capitalism's mad ravenous addiction to growth, the three little pigs survived in the house made of earthen bricks.

People overrate their ability to perceive and remember faces they saw only once. Jed Rakoff (New York Review of Books (4/18/2019) points out that eyewitnesses in courtrooms are frequently wrong. The Innocence Project studied 360 cases that were overturned by DNA evidence.

- Inaccurate eyewitness identifications   70% of the time
- Misleadng expert testimony   45% of the time
- False confessions   30% of the time

And, it is difficult for jurors to sort things out because they are as vulnerable to fallacy as everyone else in the courtroom.

Robert Porter said of himself:
- I have a Buddhist brain
- I have a Jewish heart
- I have a pagan body

<u>Immoderate Greatness - Why Civilizations Fail</u>, by **W**illiam Olphus, has a quote by Joseph Tainter commenting on how, for the past 12,000 years, humans have negotiated the vast increase in the complexity of their societies. Most people approve of this increase because of all the benefits it brings to them, but societies must pay the ultimate price for the complexity as our easier solutions are exhausted and our problem solving moves us inexorably to:

- Greater complexity
- Higher costs
- Diminishing returns.

Olphus wrote that simply maintaining our level of complexity in infrastructure, in regulation, and in expertise begins to consume more and more resources:
- Human resources
- Capital resources
- Material resources

Thus, society will have to run harder and harder just to stay in place.

Harari discussed the different ways pre-modern and modern societies deal with the triadic formations in the social structure of individuals, communities, and the state:

Pre-modern:
- Strong families and communities lead to a weak state and market (we'll make it ourselves; let the Hatfields and McCoys duke it out themselves)
- Weak protections lead to weak individuals
- Weak individuals then depend on strong families and communities

Modern:
- Weak families and communities lead to the need for a strong state and market which empowers individuals to pay their own taxes and to "be all that they can be"
- Strong state protections and services lead to strong individuals
- Strong individuals no longer depend on strong families and communities, so people marry who they want and people move around without resistance

"Leaves of three, let it be", A dictum to keep in mind for avoiding some annoying itching and scratching.

The *trivium*, the three medieval branches of knowledge whose study led to the Bachelor of Arts degree:
- Grammar
- Logic
- Rhetoric

Fritjof Capra mentions this in his book, <u>The Science of Leonardo.</u>

$$3 \times 3 \times 3 = 27$$

There are twenty-seven cubes in a stack of sugar cubes, whose dimensions are three sugar cubes wide by three sugar cubes long by three sugar cubes deep. Bing! A memory... my grandmother would lean against the warm clanging steaming radiator on a cold winter morning sipping tea in the Russian style with a sugar cube in her mouth.

Gaia Vince remarks in her book, <u>Transcendence</u>, that we took a wild auroch and guided its evolution to produce a domesticated cow. We drank its milk and our genes adapted. This is evolution:
- by means of cultural processes
- by environmental changes
- by genetic adaptions

Capra wrote that in the 15th century the terms "art" and "science" had different meanings. Art meant "skill" and science meant "knowledge." Capra gives Leonardo's synthesis of what is needed to be an artist:

- *Arte*
- *Sciente*
- *Fantasia*, or the artistic creative imagination.

Brandon Payne, the private trainer for the great basketball player, Stephen Curry, employs a regimen that has his players work on:

- Acceleration
- Deceleration
- Stability

The "Three Sisters," provided the people of Mesoamerica a complete nutrient triangle since each contributes a good part of the vitamin mix human beings need. Furthermore, planting these three together helps to retain nutrients in the soil:

- Maize or corn was domesticated about 5000 B.C.E.
- Squash was cultivated as early as 1000 B.C.E.
- Beans, which were also used very early.

221

Three social-political slogans inflaming passions and raising hackles in the second decade of the 21st century:

- Medicare for all
- Black Lives Matter
- Make America Great Again

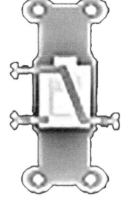

normal switch

3-way switch

A variation of the standard *single-pole* switch is a three-way wall switch that makes it possible to control a ceiling light or other electrical fixture from two different locations in a room. In a hallway or large room, for example, installing three-way switches at both ends lets you turn the light fixture on or off from both locations.

Annamalai Swami, a devotee of Ramana Maharshi said that though his guru seems to have given three paths to enlightenment:

- Path of self-inquiry
- Path of observation of the breath
- Path of diving within the heart

The three paths were essentially three ways of describing the same thing. Self-inquiry is trying to find out who you really are. Who Am I? Who am I? Who am I? The question is not repeated as a mantra but always kept in mind and being. I am not the body. I am not the mind. Such answers in words are not the "Answer" either. Ramana said the source of the breath and the source of the mind are the same, so following the second path of breath awareness is similar. Their source is in the spiritual Heart which is the essence of the third path. Annamalai Swami - mind, he said, only gets dissolved in the Self by constant practice. Note, that the goal is the capital "S" Self, the Christos, Nirvana, and Zen of all the spiritual paths and not the "self" featured on magazines at the checkout counter. See the book by David Godman, Annamalai Swami Final Talks.

Heidegger and other people on his Western Philosophy team slice things in a dualist way. Eugene T. Gendlin, in his article "An Analysis of Martin Heidegger's <u>What is a Thing</u>?" (www.focusing.org/gendlin/docs/gol_2041.html) writes that "Heidegger goes beyond Kant and other philosophers, for he begins with the ordinary things around us. To be more accurate, he begins with us and the things around us, as we are among them at this time in history." Heidegger sets up three categories:

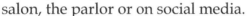

- Objects around us
- Human attitudes and procedures
- Totality of these two in interdependence together

Nisargadatta, Ramana Maharshi, and the Oneness teachers just merge with the Totality. They are not interested in setting up a thinking game in the journal, the salon, the parlor or on social media.

The reality Ramana Maharshi taught is:

- One Self
- One Life
- One Existence

In a 21st century version of *advaita*, Oneness teacher Rupert Spira wrote

- Only awareness
- Is aware
- Of awareness.

- Only being aware
- Is being aware of
- being aware.

Although these *mahavakyas* (*maha* = great, *vakya* = statement) are made of words, they must be contemplated, felt, and sensed beyond the words, the dust bunnies floating in the mind, and the whole mind itself. Is this "awareness" the answer to Ramana's "Who am I?" question? I am the awareness of experience; the same "I" I was as a child, the same field of awareness as ever and the same "I" and the same field of awareness as everyone else's. This awareness is prayer and divinity, says Spira. It's the truth. It's actual, and it's satisfactual." It's *sat, chit, and ananda*. Is this the best thing since white bread? I hope so, I'm working on it.

Ramana speaks from his direct experience. He also quotes the 8th-century sage, Shankaracharya, who said:

- Brahman is real
- The Universe is unreal
- Brahman is the Universe.

Huh? What he means is the universe is real if perceived as the Self and unreal if perceived apart from the Self. Hence, Ramana says, Maya and Reality are one and the same thing. (*S.S. Cohen in his book, <u>Guru Ramana</u>*)

"When the mind is lost in supreme awareness, all three drives:

- desiring
- doing
- knowing

are seen as conceptual movements in the Self", wrote the poet Sri Muruganar, a disciple of Ramana Maharshi in his book, <u>The Garland of the Guru's Sayings</u>.

Thai master, Buddhadasa said the mind leads and the body is merely the tool that is led. He said that what we call "mind" is very:

- Subtle
- Complex
- Profound

David Godman, author of <u>The Teachings of Ramana Maharshi</u>, wrote that the master indicated three classes of spiritual seekers:

- The most advanced realize the Self immediately after hearing the truth.
- The second class require some time of reflection before the Self is realized.
- The less fortunate ones in the last category require many years of intense spiritual practice to reach Self-realization.

Ramana used the metaphor of combustion to describe the three levels:

- Gunpowder ignites with a single spark
- Charcoal needs the application of heat and fanning for some time before it ignites
- Wet coal needs to be dried out before it can be lit. This seems like my level and most of the other human beings I know and, alas, the drying out period can possibly take lifetimes.

Three powers of the Divine:

- Omniscience
- Omnipresence
- Omnipotence

Nisargadatta Maharaj was a great Oneness teacher who died in 1981 at age 84. He lived in a poor neighborhood of Bombay, supporting his family by manufacturing *beedis*, a local Indian cigarette. He said, "…in reality all is the One;

- Observed
- Observation
- Observer

are mental constructs. "The Self alone is." His wisdom is profound and can be gleaned in a book of conversations he held with Westerners that has been translated into many languages. It is called, <u>I Am That</u>. He never studied quantum mechanics, but he did say, "The very fact of observation alters the observer and the observed." And continuing on this theme, he said," What is observable is not the real Self." As for reality, he said, "…it is obvious that everything is the cause of everything, that everything is as it is because the entire universe is as it is." And he also said, "There is only life, there is nobody who lives life." An instruction he give for working on your mind is, " Watch your thoughts like street traffic."

In his book, <u>Gleanings From Nisargadatta,</u> Mark West gives Maharaj's ordering of Reality:

- Awareness
- Consciousness (God, creator, consciousness of I AM)
- Body/World

Maharaj said, "Pure awareness does not admit to anything of individuality. When consciousness comes, then individuality appears. It is all a dream within awareness. Awareness is the sole reality. Anyone who fully understands this is called an avatar."

Nisargadatta Maharaj said:
"Delayed response is wrong response.

- Thought
- Feeling
- Action

must be one and simultaneous with the situation that calls for them." compiled by Robert Powell in his book, <u>The Nectar of Immortality,</u> Sri <u>Nisargadatta Maharaj's Discourses on the Eternal</u>

Thich Nhat Hanh concludes his commentary on the "Heart Sutra" by saying that there are three kinds of gifts:
- The gift of material stuff
- The gift of knowledge
- The highest gift of all, the gift of no-fear.

The Heart Sutra concludes with the mantra:

gate gate paragate parasamgate bodhi svaha
Gone, gone, gone all the way,
everyone gone to the other shore,
enlightenment,
Hallelujah
Yes Sireee Bob

Cancer treatment for the past century has involved three basic treatments:
- surgery to take out tumors
- radiation to burn out the tumors
- chemotherapy to poison the tumors

The Nobel Prize for medicine in 2018 was awarded to James P. Allison and Tasuku Honjo for their discoveries of how to get the body to cure the cancers with its own immune system. Jerome Groopman explains the new therapies in his article "The Body Strikes Back" (New York Review of Books 2/21/2019) as he reviews two books, <u>An Elegant Defense: The Extraordinary New Science of the Immune System</u> by Matt Richtel and <u>The Beautiful Cure: The Revolution in Immunology and What It Means for Your Health</u> by Daniel M. Davis. Groopman writes "our immune system is restrained from attacking tumors by molecules that function as 'brakes'. Releasing these brakes allows our body to powerfully combat cancer." The new therapies, which are not perfect, inhibit "blockers" so that the immune system's cells can go to work.

It really is One, like the ocean with all its
- Tides
- Ripples
- Waves. *The Ashtavakra Gita verse 2-4*

Watch out! "There is a lack of wisdom in the wave who thinks it's not a part of the larger ocean," says Rupert Spira.

Consider the love and compassion of the "Mother of the Universe" as She creates this Oneness out of Her own Being. This is one of the Hindu parsings of creation.

An ancient Greek formulation has three primordial entities: (see Luc Ferry's book: The Wisdom of the Myths)
- Chaos
- Gaia
- Eros

With "Gaia giving birth under the impetus of Eros, all alone, without husband or lover, out of her own depths and her own resources to a formidably powerful god, Uranus, the starry sky." Uranus and Gaia then procreate the pantheon of all the other gods and the material world.

In a leaner formulation, Lao Tzu said that the Tao gives birth to one, one gives - birth to two, two gives birth to three, and three gives birth to the ten thousand things ...

Afterward

This book could easily have kept going on and on. After all, it's a collection of short articles and pictorial content scented with the "threeness" that wafts about everywhere all the time. The message here is, there's nothing special about "threeness". We could produce a series. We could make books on "twoness", "fourness", "fiveness," etc.

Can we "see" any reality to "threeness?" First, let's ask a deeper question. What reality do we "see" in laws of science? This question was discussed in a conversation between Albert Einstein and Rabindranath Tagore, the Nobel Prize-winning Indian poet, on July 14, 1930, at Einstein's house near Berlin. (It's out there, Google it.) Tagore's point of view was that Truth is human and comes with the realization of Oneness. Einstein believed that there is Truth independent of man. He gives the example of the Pythagorean theorem which states a truth about space and the relationship between the sum of the lengths of the short sides of a right triangle and the measure of the hypotenuse or long side, remember $(A^2+B^2=C^2)$.

Point of disclosure: I've studied physics and I've taken "the journey to the East." I tend to side with Tagore, but I don't have too much patience with New Age happy horse whinny.

Back to Tagore and Einstein. I've never seen a dog go in a straight line. The only "straight lines" I've ever experienced are man-made. The concept of a straight line is man-made. Science is made of man-made measurements organized into laws and theories. Practical, no doubt. I've got a pacemaker embedded in my chest. "E" does equal "M" times "C" squared as shown at Hiroshima. Google Maps are accurate because GPS systems obey the laws of relativity theory!

Science sees the world through the glasses of the measurable. To believe that this is the ultimate truth is also happy horse whinny. Marcelo Gleiser emphatically wrote about the limits of science and its search for meaning in The Island of Knowledge, an island in the vast ocean of the unknown.

"My deep intuitions, spoken to me by my revelatory angels, are beyond the measurable," said a New Age blogger. This is happy horse whinny too.

One of the *mahavakyas* (great sayings) from the Vedas is, *Neti Neti* (Not This, Not This) Reality is not what you say it is and it's not not what you say it is.

Abraham Joshua Heschel spoke of "Wonder, Awe, and Radical Amazement" in the mid-20th-century. After I got my Ph.D., I would sit on the California cliffs watching the waves come in and exclaim, "Look at that wave, it is totally infinitely wonderful. The laws of physics cannot capture its infinite nature." The laws of physics can only do the accounting: the heights, the speeds, the volumes, the numbers per hour; stuff that can be put in a spreadsheet. With engineering, increased precision brought about the manifestation of new phenomena and digital gizmos. The early 20th-century philosopher, Heidegger, said that we now live beyond nature in the techno-sphere.

Is there any Truth to "threeness?" Among the Wiccans, Rosicrucians, astrologers, Gurdjieffiens, Rudolph Steiner acolytes, Theosophists, Trinitarians, practitioners of Ayurvedic medicine, and some mystical people here and there, the archetype of "three" lubricates their psyches, logics, and sciences to help inform the way they see the world…and who knows the inner workings and mysteries in the cults of the Triplicarians, Trioists, and Triadians.

Is there a truth to "seventeenness?" Among members of the theoretical physicist community in the mid-twentieth century, seventeen was their most popular random number.

Finally, about "Oneness": those who live knowingly immersed in and aware of the One are the Oneness teachers. I myself, author of this book, am not a Oneness teacher. I can only point to Oneness teachers. I live in Oneness like just about everyone else and, like most others, realize it only in specs of time.

Meanwhile, watch out! There are "word-slicers" who, masquerading as Oneness teachers, turn only their words to oneness. They can start anywhere, slice the deck, slice it again, and within six slices they wind up at a oneness. Grief, tragedy, suffering...slice, slice, slice...no matter, it's all one.

There is mystery. Duality practiced with a pure heart is closer to Oneness than "wordy oneness." Someone praying to God is practicing duality. Mahalia Jackson does this. Listen to her sing "Just a Closer Walk With Thee," and feel how she's merged her being into the One.

Black Elk, the Oglala Sioux shaman, spoke about the first peace which "comes within the souls of people when they realize their relationship, their oneness with the universe, and all its powers, and when they realize that at the center of the universe dwells the Great Spirit, and that this center is really everywhere, it is within each of us."

Ramana Maharshi said "...Truth shines as the Formless Perfection and the substratum of the world." To Ramana, a person living in Oneness is said to have realized the Self. Here is his full quote: "To those who have not realized the Self as well as to those who have, the world is real, but to the former (scientists included) Truth is adapted to the form of the world whereas to the later, Truth shines as the Formless Perfection and the substratum of the world." Would that we all realize this Truth.

Love-Surrender-Faith
Object-Thought-Emotion
Things-Substances-Entities
Waking-Dream-Deep Sleep
Knowledge-Knower-Known
Perceiving-Thinking-Feeling
Events-Happenings-Processes
Feudalism-Capitalism-Dataism
Observed-Observation-Observer
One Caste-One God-One Religion
One Self-One Life-One existence
Measurer-Measured-Measuring
The Way-The Truth-The Life
Equality-Freedom-Justice
Thought-Feeling-Action
Body-Mind-Intellect
Truth-Peace-Justice
Mass-Length-Time
Race-Color-Creed
World-Soul-God
Sight-Seer-Seen

231

Bibliography

Adams, Robert	Silence of the Heart
Adams, Robert	Silence of the Heart
Asimov, Isaac	I, Robot
Aslan, Reza	No god but God
Balsekar, Ramesh	A Duet of One
	commentary on the Ashtavakra Gita
Batchelor, Stephen	Buddhism Without Beliefs
Baum, Frank	Wizard of Oz
Blumrosen, Alfred and Ruth	Slave Nation:
	"How Slavery United The Colonies And Sparked The American Revolution"
Bobrick, Benson	Caliph's Splendor
Borgman, Albert	Holding On to Reality
	"The Nature of Information at the Turn of the Millennium"
Burton, Robert A.	On Being Certain
Burton, Robert A.	A Skeptic's Guide to the Mind
Capra, Fritjof	The Science of Leonardo
Carroll, James	Christ Actually
Chodron, Pema	This Moment Is the Perfect Teacher
Chodron, Pema	The Wisdom of No Escape
Chomsky, Noam and Herman, Edward S.	Manufacturing of Consent
Coates, Ta-Nehisi	We Were Eight Years in Power
Cohen, S.S.	Guru Ramana
Dattatreya the sage	Tripuri Rahasya
Damasio, Antonio	Looking for Spinoza
Damasio, Antonio	Descartes Error
Damasio, Antonio	The Strange Order of Things
	"Life, Feeling, and the Making of Cultures."
Damasio, Antonio	The Feeling of What Happens.
	"Body and Emotion in the Making of Consciousness"
Domingos, Pedro	The Master Algorithm
Dyson, George	Darwin Among the Machines
Engel, Susan	The Hungry Mind:
	The Origins of Curiosity in Childhood
Feiler, Bruce	Abraham
Ferry, Luc	A Brief History of Thought
FitzGerald, Frances	The Evangelicals: The Struggle to Shape America
Frankl, Victor	Man's Search for Meaning
Forbes, Nancy and Mahon, Basil	Faraday, Maxwell, and the Electromagnetic Field
Foundation for Inner Peace	A Course in Miracles
	The Key to Success in Life
Freire, Paulo	Pedagogy of the Oppressed
Galeano, Eduardo	Mirrors
Gazzaniga, Michael	Who's In Charge
Gleiser, Marcelo	The Island of Knowledge
Godman, David	Anamalai Swami Final Talks
Godman, David	The Teachings of Ramana Maharsh
Goldstein, Joseph	Mindfulness

Harari, Yuval Noah   Sapiens
Harari, Yuval Noah   21 Lessons for the 21st Century
Heidegger, Martin   What is a Thing?
Herman, Arthur   The Cave and the Light
Hochschild, Arlie Russell   Strangers in a Strange Land
                              "Anger and Mourning on the American Right"
Hudson, Michael   Killing the Host
                            "How Financial Parasites and Debt Bondage Destroy the Global Economy"
Huxley, Aldous   Brave New World
Keen, Andrew   The Internet is Not the Answer
Klein, Jean   Who Am I - The Sacred Quest
Klein, Jean   Be What You Are
Lester, Julius   Sam and the Tigers:
                              A New Telling of Little Black Sambo
Lustic, Robert   The Hacking of the American Mind
MacLean, Paul   The Triune Brain in Evolution
Mitchell, Stephen (editor) The Enlightened Mind
Moss, Michael   Salt Sugar Fat: How the Food Giant Hooked Us
Muruginar, Sri   The Garland of Guru's Sayings
                            Guru Vachaka Kovai
                            translated by Sri Sadhu Om and Michael James
Nisargadatta   I Am That
Ohler, Norman   Blitzed: Drugs in the Third Reich
Osborne, Arthur (editor)   Collected Works of Ramana Maharshi
Oz, Amos & Oz-Salzberger, Fania   Jews and Words
Paramahansa Yogananda   Wine of the Mystic
Parsons, Tony   As It Is
Powell, John A.   Racing to Justice
Ricard, Mathieu   Altruism:
                              The Power of Compassion to Change Yourself and the World
Robinson, Duke   A Middle Way
                              "The Secular/Spiritual Road to Wholeness"
Rovelli, Carlo   The Order of Time
Rovelli, Carlo   Seven Brief Lessons On Physics
Rovelli, Carlo   Reality Is Not What It Seems
Schlain, Leonard   The Alphabet Versus the Goddess:
                              The Conflict Between Word and Image
Schlain, Leonard   Sex, Time and Power:
                              How Women's Sexuality Shaped Human Evolution
Sofer, Oren Jay   say what you mean
                              a mindful approach to nonviolent communication
Stanley, Jason   How Fascism Works
Stone, I.F.   The Trial of Socrates
Sunstein, C   #Republic: Divided Democracy in the Age of Social Media
Swami Chinmayananda   Ashtavakra Gita   (A Commentary)
                              translated at Ramakrishna Ashram)
Swami Ramakrishnananda Puri Amritastakam
Tarnas, Richard   Passion Of the Western Mind
Thich Nhat Hanh   How to Sit
Thich Nhat Hanh   The Heart of the Buddha's Teaching
Thich Nhat Hanh   Understanding Our Mind
Thich Nhat Hanh   No Mud No Lotus
Trungpa, Chögyam   Woek Sex Money

Godman, David   Anamalai Swami Final Talks
Godman, David   The Teachings of Ramana Maharsh
Goldstein, Joseph   Mindfulness
Harari, Yuval Noah   Sapiens
Harari, Yuval Noah   21 Lessons for the 21st Century
Heidegger, Martin   What is a Thing?
Herman, Arthur   The Cave and the Light
Hochschild, Arlie Russell   Strangers in a Strange Land
                            "Anger and Mourning on the American Right"

Hudson, Michael   Killing the Host
                            "How Financial Parasites and Debt Bondage Destroy the Global Economy"

Huxley, Aldous   Brave New World
Keen, Andrew   The Internet is Not the Answer
Klein, Jean   Who Am I - The Sacred Quest
Klein, Jean   Be What You Are
Lester, Julius   Sam and the Tigers:
                            A New Telling of Little Black Sambo

Levinson, Lester   Keys to the Ultimate Freedom
Lustic, Robert   The Hacking of the American Mind
MacLean, Paul   The Triune Brain in Evolution
Mitchell, Stephen (editor)   The Enlightened Mind
Moss, Michael   Salt Sugar Fat: How the Food Giant Hooked Us
Muruginar, Sri   The Garland of Guru's Sayings
                            Guru Vachaka Kovai
                            translated by Sri Sadhu Om and Michael James

Nisargadatta   I Am That
Ohler, Norman   Blitzed: Drugs in the Third Reich
Osborne, Arthur (editor)   Collected Works of Ramana Maharshi
Oz, Amos & Oz-Salzberger, Fania   Jews and Words
Paramahansa Yogananda   Wine of the Mystic
Parsons, Tony   As It Is
Peace Pilgrim   Peace Pilgrim Her Life and Work in Her Own Words
Powell, John A.   Racing to Justice
Prasada, Rama   Patanjali's Yoga Sutras
Ricard, Mathieu   Altruism:
                            The Power of Compassion to Change Yourself and the World

Robinson, Duke   A Middle Way
                            "The Secular/Spiritual Road to Wholeness"

Rovelli, Carlo   The Order of Time
Rovelli, Carlo   Seven Brief Lessons On Physics
Rovelli, Carlo   Reality Is Not What It Seems
Schlain, Leonard   <u>The Alphabet Versus the Goddess:</u>
                            The Conflict Between Word and Image

Schlain, Leonard   <u>Sex, Time and Power:</u>
                            How Women's Sexuality Shaped Human Evolution

Sofer, Oren Jay   say what you mean
                            a mindful approach to nonviolent communication

Spira, Rupert   Being Aware of Being Aware
Stanley, Jason   How Fascism Works
Stone, I.F.   The Trial of Socrates
Sunstein, C   #Republic: Divided Democracy in the Age of Social Media
Swami Chinmayananda   Ashtavakra Gita   (A Commentary)
                            translated at Ramakrishna Ashram)
Swami Ramakrishnananda Puri   Amritastakam

Graphics Acknowledgements

A major source for the graphics in this book are photographs, drawings and renderings by the author. The other sources are images in the public domain mostly download from the internet. This second group is annotated below.

The graphics are listed by the number of the page on which they appear. For multiple graphics on the same page, say page 17, they are listed as 17A, 17B, 17C... where 17A appears highest on the page

28A   https://unsplash.com/photos/71CjSSB83Wo Photo by Pavan Trikutam on Unsplash
3 pay phones

30B   Christopher_Santa_Mar%C3%ADa_-_Pinta_-_Ni%C3%B1a.jpg
Appletons' Cyclopædia of American Biography, 1900, v. 1, p. 697
Nina, Pinta, & Santa Maria

34B   https://commons.wikimedia.org/wiki/File:Three-
msasted_ship_KING_GEORGE_at_anchor,_Washington,_ca_1900_(HESTER_588).jpeg
University of Washington   **three-master**

41   https://commons.wikimedia.org/wiki/File:Andrej_Rubl%C3%ABv_001.jpg
CCO   Russian iconographer and monk   **3 Angels Andrej Rublëv**
circa early 1400s   located at Tretyakov Gallery

44A   https://www.maxpixel.net/Terrarium-Snake-Venomous-Animals-Camo-Bastards-
1519983   **3 snakes**   CC0 Public Domain from maxpixel.net

44B   https://commons.wikimedia.org/wiki/File:The_three_musketeers_fairbanks.jpg
this media file is in the public domain in the United States   From the movie poster starring
Douglas Fairbanks   **3 musketeers**

45A   ivana-cajina-424716-unsplash.com   **3 people at the seashore**

47B
https://www.google.com/search?hl=en&biw=1268&bih=529&tbm=isch&sa=1&ei=FB9GXcCPGcz
Z-gSGoYWQCg&q=elcarito-1493208-unsplash.jpg+++++&oq=elcarito-1493208-
unsplash.jpg+++++&gs_l=img.12...48117.48117..49589...0.0..0.69.69.1......0....2j1..gws-wiz-
img.ljIyJu67AxQ&ved=0ahUKEwjA6fS98-fjAhXMrJ4KHYZQAaIQ4dUDCAY#imgrc=wfYrEOOZosmqtM:
elcarito-1493208-unsplash.jpg   **3 ostriches** photo by El Carito

48A   https://commons.wikimedia.org/wiki/File:Cute_Sloth.jpg   author is Epicawesomewolf
creative commons   **3 toed sloth**

50A   https://commons.wikimedia.org/wiki/File:Allegories_of_Faith,_Hope,_and_Charity_MET_DP80
4345.jpg   **Allegories of Faith, Hope, and Charity** by Heinrich Maria Von Hess (1798-1863)

50B
https://www.google.com/search?hl=en&biw=1268&bih=529&tbm=isch&sa=1&ei=Rh9GXaabKZf
m-gTTpIXQDw&q=david-heslop-609112-unsplash&oq=david-heslop-609112-
unsplash&gs_l=img.12...107046.107046..110027...0.0..0.75.75.1......0....2j1..gws-wiz-
img.VPm6n27FoSY&ved=0ahUKEwim1vDV8-
fjAhUXs54KHVNSAfoQ4dUDCAY#imgrc=ZeyQcVDv2K183M: **3 puffins**   david-heslop-609112-unsplash

51A   https://commons.wikimedia.org/wiki/File:Bonampak_Painting.jpg   **Mayan wall painting**

52   https://pxhere.com/en/photo/550449   **jump rope mural** cco public domain

53B   from Japanese screen at the Met   **3 myna birds**

55A   an-shin.net/Hongseong-Yongbong-YBsa3SG.html The Samseong-gak of Hongseong Yongbong-sa
Temple of the 3 sages by permission of David Mason

56A   an-shin.net/Hongseong-Yongbong-YBsa3SG.html The Samseong-gak of Hongseong Yongbong-sa
Temple of the 3 sages by permission of David Mason

60A   https://commons.wikimedia.org/wiki/File:ClavisArtis.Ms-2-27.Hortis.V3.039.jpg   dragon
Zoroaster Clavis Artis, Ms-2-27, **3 headed dragon** Biblioteca Civica Hortis, Trieste

61A   https://commons.wikimedia.org/wiki/File:ClavisArtis.Ms-2-27.Hortis.V3.034.jpg   dragon
Zoroaster Clavis Artis, Ms-2-27, **3 headed dragon** Biblioteca Civica Hortis, Trieste

62A   https://www.pikrepo.com/febtq/three-gray-elephants-on-ground/download **3 elephants**

63B   https://commons.wikimedia.org/wiki/File:Six_Heads,_Three_Feet,_Two_Ears,_Six_Eyes,_Four_
Lips_MET_DP819528.jpg   Battista Franco Veneziano (1510–1561) Met NYC **3 heads**

65A
    http://www.getty.edu/art/collection/objects/247408/unknown-maker-the-three-maries-at-the-
sepulchre-english-about-1190-1200-text-and-illumination-added-about-1480-1490/   **3 Maries at the
Sepulchre** English about 1190–1200; text and illumination added about 1480–1490
Object Number: Ms. 101 (2008.3), fol. 81

70B   KoreanSages7 Stars Alter.jpg an-shin.net/Hongseong-Yongbong-YBsa3SG.html The Samseong-
gak of Hongseong Yongbong-**sa** **Temple of the 3 sages** by permission of David Mason

71A   https://www.metmuseum.org/art/collection/search/209270   the Met NYC
The Three Graces by Pinturissio 1509

75B   https://commons.wikimedia.org/wiki/File:Edgar_Degas_-_Three_Dancers_in_Red_Costume_-
_Google_Art_Project.jpg   Three Dancers in Red Costume Edgar Degas Ohara Museum of Art

77A   **3 Terracotta female figures** The Met NYC

80   **From an Egyptian mural at the Metropolitan Museum** of Art,NYC

81A   https://unsplash.com/photos/8w_cqjcDRC4 **3 sadhus** by Sebastian Pena Lambarri

81B
Theee_women_tiredly_look_at_Antoin_Sevruguin_as_he_photographs_them_in_the_late_19th_ce
ntury..jpeg
Wikimedia Commons, the free media repository Antonin Sevruguin (1830s-1933) Iran

84A   https://pixabay.com/photos/vendors-women-traditional-street-3555692/

    3 Chinese fruit vendors

84B   https://www.pexels.com/photo/adult-art-ballerina-ballet-209948
3 ballerinas Creative Common Image

85A   a small section of a **Jackson Pollock painting** hanging at the Met NYC   City

89A   https://commons.wikimedia.org/wiki/File:Standing_Alaskan_Coastal_Brown_bear.jpg
Standing **Alaskan Coastal Brown bear**.jpg photo by Alan Vernon

    https://commons.wikimedia.org/wiki/File:**Fox**_-_British_Wildlife_Centre_(7061186471).jpg
British Wildlife Centre (7061186471).jpg photo by Peter Trimming

    https://www.goodfreephotos.com/animals/mammals/another-bunny.jpg.php **Another Bunny
at Nine Springs** Natural Area, Madison, Wisconsin

90   https://commons.wikimedia.org/wiki/File:Wynken,_Blynken,_and_Nod.png

fromJohnson's first-(fifth) reader 1899 **Winkin', Blikin', & Nod**

94B   http://www.getty.edu/art/collection/objects/240661/unknown-maker-the-creation-of-the-
animals-and-of-adam-and-eve-english-about-1250-1260/?dz=0.5000,0.5000,0.50
The Creation of the Animals and of Adam and Eve English 1250–1260
Object Number: Ms. 100 (2007.16), fol. 3v   J. Paul Getty Museum

95A   https://commons.wikimedia.org/wiki/File:Egipto,_1882_%22Isis,_Osiris,_Horus%22_(2167456021
5).jpg   **Isis, Osiris, Horus** Ilustrator:Werner, Karl, 1821-1888,

95B   https://picryl.com/media/joe-tinker-chicago-cubs-baseball-card-portrait-2
copyright public do main Library of Congress   **Tinker to Evans to Chance**

96B   Gauguin's Three Tahitian Women 1896 Metropolitan Museum of Art

97   https://commons.wikimedia.org/wiki/File:Troisordres.jpg Bibliothèque nationale de France
3 orders of society

99   Claude Mellan (1598-1688)
Three Graces Met NYC public domain

100A   **Ethiopian Illuminated Gospel** 14th-15th century
Metropolitan Museum of Art NYC

100B   https://commons.wikimedia.org/wiki/File:Three_hula_dancers_with_ukulele._Lizzie_Puahi_in_c
enter_(PP-32-9a-017).jpg
File:Three hula dancers, Lizzie Puahi in center (PP-32-8-018).jpg Wikimedia Commons
Hawaii State Archives. Call Number: PP-32-8-018   **Hula Dancers**

101   **Jamini Roy** (1887-1972) commons.wikimedia.org/wiki/File:Boating_(6124606361).jpg
The San Diego Museum of Art

103a   **Jamani Roy** (1887-1972) from the collection Dr. Nural Kumarand with his permission

103B   **Jamani Roy** (1887-1972) from the collection Dr. Nural Kumarand with his permission

103C   https://commons.wikimedia.org/wiki/File:Chhath-Puja-Bihar.jpg **Chhath Puja of Bihar**
photographer is Cpjha13, This file is licensed under the Creative Commons Attribution-Share Alike
4.0 International license

1105B   **Jamani Roy** (1887-1972) from the collection Dr. Nural Kumarand with his permission

104   https://awazo.com/article/three_men_in_a_shop.html
3 Men in a shop #6437   Malsa India by Tetsu Ozawa at 'https://awazo.com'.

108   https://commons.wikimedia.org/wiki/File:Wine_Women_and_Song_poster.jpg
1933 movie author is I.E. Chadwick Wine, Women, & Song

109   https://commons.wikimedia.org/wiki/File:1952.27-Three_dancing_nymphs-SBMA.jpg
File:1952.27-Three dancing nymphs-SBMA.jpg 1952.27 (Santa Barbara Museum of Art)
photographer Christelle Molinié   **3 dancing nymphs**

110A   **Eat, drink, and be merry**
https://commons.wikimedia.org/wiki/File:Master_of_the_Dresden_Prayer_Book_(Flemish,_activ
e_about_1480_-_1515)_-_The_Temperate_and_the_Intemperate_-_Google_Art_Project.jpg

110B   3 youngHipAsians.jpg 3https://www.maxpixel.net/Asia-Three-Character-Young-Inspirational-1160200   CC0 Public Domain from maxpixel.net

111   File:Edmund J Sullivan Illustrations to The Rubaiyat of Omar Khayyam First Version Quatrain-010.jpg https://commons.wikimedia.org/wiki/   **A loaf of bread, a jug of wine, and thou**
_The_Temperate_and_the_Intemperate_-_Google_Art_Project.jpg

114   https://commons.wikimedia.org/wiki/File:Sandro_Botticelli_-_Three_Graces_in_Primavera.jpg
File:Sandro Botticelli 1445-1510- **Three Graces in Primavera**

115A   https://commons.wikimedia.org/wiki/File:Three_muslim_women_(6219047008).jpg
From Wikimedia Commons, the free media repository
Author: Emmanuel Huybrechts from Laval, Canada   CC BY 2.0
(https://creativecommons.org/licenses/by/2.0)]   **3 Muslim women**

115B   https://www.pexels.com/photo/three-women-sitting-on-bench-1267244/
3 Women drinking beers   by ELEVATE

116A   https://commons.wikimedia.org/wiki/File:Annual_catalogue_of_Jos._F._Dickmann%27s_high-class_garden,_field_and_lfower_seeds_-_seed,_grain,_implements_and_fertilizers_of_all_kinds_(1896)_(18426447541).jpg
Annual catalogue of Jos. F. Dickmann's high-class garden, field and flower seeds - seed, grain, implements and fertilizers of all kinds (1896) (18426447541).jpg   **buggies** 1896

117B   https://pixabay.com/photos/geisha-retro-vintage-japanese-asia-439318/   **3 Japanese umbrellas**

118   https://commons.wikimedia.org/wiki/File:Ernst_Ludwig_Kirchner_-_Three_bathers_-_Google_Art_Project.jpg by Ernst Ludwig Kirchner (1880– 1938)   **3 women bathers**

119   https://upload.wikimedia.org/wikipedia/commons/1/11/Károly_Ferenczy_-_Three_boys_bathing.jpg
Trois garçons de bain by Károly Ferenczy (1862–1917)   **3 young men bathing**

121   William Henry Fox Talbot Three Graces Met NYC public domain

125   https://commons.wikimedia.org/wiki/File:Hosios_Loukas_(diakonikon)_-_Fiery_furnace_01.jpg
Shadrach, Meshach, & Abednego

126   https://commons.wikimedia.org/wiki/File:Three_Sisters_cover_1901.jpg   The front cover of the first edition of **Three Sisters by Chekov** published 1901 by Adolf Marks, St Petersburg

127A   https://www.pexels.com/photo/adult-book-business-desk-1181617/
by Christina Morilloi **3 women at conference table**

128B
https://www.britishmuseum.org/research/collection_online/collection_object_details.aspx?objectId=1397590&partId=1&searchText=three+men&page=6
File:Albrecht Dürer - Three Peasants in Conversation - WGA7276.jpg   **3 men by Albrecht Durer**
Museum number1910,0212.306   Date 1497 Metropolitan Museum New York

133   https://commons.wikimedia.org/wiki/File:William_Blake_-_Dante_running_from_the_three_beasts_Google_Art_Project.jpg
from a painting by **William Blake(three beasts)**

134A   *from a Japanese Screen a*t the Met by an Unknown Artist

134B   **from a Japanese Screen** at the Met by an Unknown Artist

*135   Maiden mother crone composite
135B   collage of 3 sources: from left to right
Maiden: Peasant Girl With Sheep by Julien Dupré 1895 Palace of Legion of Honor San Francisco
Mother: https://commons.wikimedia.org/wiki/File:**Pregnant_woman_**(1).jpg
          Author: Meagan from Tulsa, OK, United States
Crone: https://commons.wikimedia.org/wiki/File:**Old_zacatecas_lady**.jpg
          This file was a candidate in Picture of the Year 2007.
          This is a featured picture on Wikimedia Commons Old lady from Zacatecas, Mexico
          Author: Tomas Castelazo

136A   http://www.getty.edu/art/collection/objects/88785/henry-pointer-three-men-posing-with-three-white-horses-british-about-1868/   Henry Pointer (British, 1822 - 1889) 3 men with three white horses 1868,
84.XC.873.5888   The J. Paul Getty Museum, Los Angeles

137   https://commons.wikimedia.org/wiki/File:Three_zebras_(6073137479).jpg
          by Derek Keats from Johannesburg, South Africa   **3 zebras**

139B   -https://pixabay.com/photos/egyptian-art-detail-three-men-1692989/   Image
by kerttu from Pixabay   **3 ancient Egyptian men**

140   Wall painting on Sacramento St. a few blocks east of Polk St. in Fan Francisco

141   https://commons.wikimedia.org/wiki/File:Animals_of_the_past_BHL18007243.jpg
          https://www.biodiversitylibrary.org/pageimage/18007243   **3 horned dinosaur**

143   https://www.pexels.com/photo/alternative-energy-blade-clouds-ecology-243138/
          photographer: Sam Forson   **wind energy**

144   https://upload.wikimedia.org/wikipedia/commons/8/8a/3_windmills.JPG
          File:3 windmills.JPG From Wikimedia Commons, the free media repository   **wind mills**

145   https://picryl.com/media/three-polo-players-f35bd5 the Met NYC CCO 3 Indian polo players

150B   https://www.metmuseum.org/art/collection/search/435809 **The Harvesters** 1565
          Metropolitan Museum of Art NYC Peter Breugel

151A   https://commons.wikimedia.org/wiki/File:Gillray-**Three-Graces-in-High-Wind**.jpg
Three-Graces-in-High-Wind.jpg a satirical engraving by James Gillray (published 1810

152   https://pxhere.com/en/photo/1111937   3 kids on trampoline

153B   https://commons.wikimedia.org/wiki/File:Scooter_family_riding,_Hubei,_China.jpg
          three on a scooter

154A   http://media.getty.edu/museum/images/web/download/08529701.jpg **Three people**
          bobsledding Artist/Maker: William Notman (Canadian, born Scotland, 1826 - 1891)
          Medium: Albumen silver print Getty Museum Los Angeles

158   https://commons.wikimedia.org/wiki/File:Giorgione_-_Three_Ages_of_Man_-_Palazzo_Pitti.jpg
          circa 1500 found at Palazzo Pitti   **3 ages of man**

161 https://upload.wikimedia.org/wikipedia/commons/c/c9/Olaus_Magnus_-
_On_Boats_that_are_put_Together_with_Sinews_and_Tree_Roots.jpg
by Olaus Magnus (1490–1557) **3 men building a boat**

162A https://dickinsonmuseumcenter.com/photo-digitization-project
drawing made from Photographer: Breum   DicksonMuseumCenter **3 men drinking beer**

162B **RubensLions.**jpg from 2019 Early Rubens show at the Palace of Fine Arts San Francisco

164A https://pixabay.com/photos/eland-male-female-three-wildlife-2483154/
by Cath Longley from Pixabay **1 male and 2 female elands**

164B from the wall painting in Babalou's Restaurant in Walnut Creek, Ca
Mahatma Ghandi, Mother Teresa, and the Dalai Lama

165A From the blog of Erin Cooper Reed https://mylifeiswear.com/2017/07/14/3-sheets-to-the-wind
3 sheets to the wind

166 https://www.pexels.com/photo/three-women-standing-near-man-holding-smartphones-
1262971/ Pexels License √ Free for personal and commercial use No attribution required
women on smart phones

168 https://commons.wikimedia.org/w/index.php?curid=490196
By Rick Dikeman - Own work, CC BY-SA 3.0, **Mark McGuire at bat**

171B
 https://commons.wikimedia.org/wiki/File:Print,_The_Three_Graces,_ca._1590_(CH_18100187).jp
g Print, **The Three Graces**, ca. 1590 (CH 18100187).jpg circa 1590 3 graces Cooper Hewitt, Smithsonian
Design Museum   Accession Number 1896-31-8

173A http://www.photos-public-domain.com/2011/11/03/**three-cats-looking-out-back-door**/ photos
public domainfree stock photos, textures, images, pictures & clipart for any use including commercial

173C
 https://commons.wikimedia.org/wiki/File:Racing_Cyclist_Mademoiselle_Lefebvre_with_cyclists
_Rousselle_and_Letort_on_a_Tandem_Bicycle_for_Three_(cropped).jpg Racing Cyclist Mademoiselle
Lefebvre with cyclists Rousselle and Letort on a **Tandem Bicycle for Three** (cropped).jpg   between 1896
and 1897 Author Jules Beau (1864–1932)

174C https://pixabay.com/de/illustrations/linie-kunst-drei-frauen-3117757/

175A https://commons.wikimedia.org/wiki/File:**Three-Women-at-the-Table**-by-the-Lamp.jpg
August Macke (1887–1914) München, Bonn, Paris, Hilterfingen am Thuner See

176B https://commons.wikimedia.org/wiki/File:Children_marbles.jpg   Photo by Tup Wanders
Children marbles.jpg

177 **Three Men at a Table** by Étienne Jeaurat 1763 at the Met NYC

178A https://commons.wikimedia.org/wiki/File:John_Downman_Witches_from_Macbeth.jpg
by John Downman (1750-1824) **3 witches from Macbeth**

180A http://www.getty.edu/art/collection/objects/88499/george-w-carter-posed-portrait-of-three-
farmers-american-about-1870/ **portrait of three farmers** by George W. Carter (American 1870)
Object Number:84.XC.1158.291 The J. Paul Getty Museum, Los Angeles

181A   https://www.metmuseum.org/art/collection/search/771145
Marcantonio Raimondi (Italian, Argini (?) ca. 1480–before 1534 Bologna   Accession
Number:31.31.44 **after Raphael's fresco** in the Chigi Gallery of the Villa Farnesina in Rome,ca.
1517–20   Met NYC

181B   https://pixabay.com/de/illustrations/frauen-wand-mauer-steine-schatten-225399/:   Image
by Gerd Altmann from Pixabay   **3 womenshadows**-225399_1920.jpg

181C   https://commons.wikimedia.org/wiki/File:The_Three_Graces,_Indianapolis_Museum_of_Art_-
_20101115.jpg   **The Three Graces**, Indianapolis Museum of Art - 20101115.jpg   circa 1920   unsigned

183A   https://commons.wikimedia.org/wiki/File:Sir_Anthony_Van_Dyck_-_Charles_I_(1600-49)_-
_Google_Art_Project.jpg   Royal Collection   **Charles 1 triple portrait**

184A   File:**Triple_Portrait_of_Cardinal_de_Richelieu**_probably_1642,_Philippe_de_Champaigne.jpg
Triple portrait of Cardinal de Richelieu, Philippe de Champaigne, c.?1642,
National Gallery, London

188   https://commons.wikimedia.org/wiki/File:**ThreeHobosChicago**1929.jpg
File:ThreeHobosChicago1929.jpg   Chicago Daily News, Library of Congress

189   **Statue of two Egyptian men and a boy** 1353-56 B.C. Metropolitan Museum NYC

192   https://commons.wikimedia.org/wiki/File:Metropolitan_mirror_3_graces_Roman_2C.jpg 3
graces
Metropolitan Museum of Art   Roman mid-2nd century AD   **3 graces on a mirror**

193   https://commons.wikimedia.org/wiki/File:Paul_Gauguin_-_Breton_Girls_Dancing,_Pont-Aven_-
_Google_Art_Project.jpg   Paul Gauguin   National Gallery of Art   **3 Breton Girls Dancing,**

194   **Blue Moon Silk Hosiery Company** circa 1920

195A   sneaky-elbow-310084-unsplash.jpg   **3 pughs**

195B   https://commons.wikimedia.org/wiki/File:Jean-Fran%C3%A7ois_Millet_(II)_002.jpg   Gleaners
Jean-François Millet   1857   Musée d'Orsay   **the gleaners by Millet**

197A   https://commons.wikimedia.org/wiki/File:Palma_il_Vecchio_-_The_Three_Sisters_(detail)_-
_WGA16928.jpg   by Palma Vecchio (1480-1528)   Old Masters Picture Gallery Dresden
                                        3 sisters

198A   https://www.pexels.com/photo/three-men-standing-in-white-uniform-and-smiling-2479942/
Photo by Brett Sayles from Pexels   **3 sailors**

200   **Three men welding an iron beam**, high above the city New York City
photo by Lewis Wickes Hines (1874-1940)   Public Library Collection

201A   **Three male singers with sheet of music** by Luca Ciamberlano 1599-1641 e Met Museum NYC

201B   dan-burton-561113-unsplash.jpg   *3 hikers*

202   https://unsplash.com/photos/G-AQWUTgMZo **3 balls of thread** Tara Evans Unsplash.com

203   https://unsplash.com/photos/G9XMLUAjETM **3 long hairdos** by Suhyeon Choi on Unsplash

204 https://commons.wikimedia.org/wiki/File:The_**Three_Graces**,_from_Pompeii.jpg
to be found in Museo Archeologico Nazionale, Naples, Italy 3 graces from Pompeii

206A **Three Women Standing on the Seashore** by Kitao Masanobu 1761–1816
at the Metropolitan Museum of Art New York City

206B http://www.getty.edu/art/collection/objects/88816/unknown-maker-three-young-male-
dancers-or-circus-performers-about-1865/ **Three young male dancers or circus performers 1865**
Object Number: 84.XC.873.5920 The J. Paul Getty Museum, LA

208A **abstracted from Sunday Morning in the Mines, 1872** Charles Christian Nahl (American, Born
Germany, 1818–1878 Crocker Art Museum, Sacramento Ca.E. B. Crocker Collection, 1872.381

208B https://unsplash.com/photos/_SB32j-cVrU
Brigitta Schneiter **3 elves**

210 https://unsplash.com/photos/GGMtP_sv6Skhoto by Tolga Ahmetler on Unsplash **3 snails**

212 https://commons.wikimedia.org/wiki/File:Giorgione_029.jpg
Kunsthistorisches_Museum A drawing from Giorgione's **Three philosophers** 1508

214 https://commons.wikimedia.org/wiki/File:KTH_Kerberos.jpg
Taken by Denoir Cerberus guarding the entrance to the Royal Institute of Technology in
Stockholm

215B https://commons.wikimedia.org/wiki/File:WhiteHouseTheThreeBillyGoatsGruff2003.jpg
This image is a work of an employee of the Executive Office of the President of the United States
3 billy goats gruff

216A a drawing made from
https://www.nasa.gov/topics/people/galleries/armstrong_may1969.html#.XJWXXShKg2w
Image Credit: NASA *3 astronauts*

216B http://www.getty.edu/art/collection/objects/90798/giorgio-conrad-three-italian-peasants-
standing-two-men-playing-wind-instruments-a-girl-next-to-them-italian-1865-1875/ 3 Italian
peasants standing: **two men playing wind instruments, a girl next to them**] Giorgio Conrad
(Italian, active 1860s) Object Number: 84.XD.1157.1426

218A https://commons.wikimedia.org/wiki/File:Hoplitodromos_Louvre_MN704.jpg
ancient Greek runners

218B section of a Chinese peasant art painting

224 https://commons.wikimedia.org/wiki/File:Erawan.JPG
Erawan, the three-headed elephant

225 https://commons.wikimedia.org/wiki/File:Angels_dancing_sun_Giovanni_di_Paolo_Cond%C3%
A9_Chantilly.jpg painting Giovanni di Paolo di Grazia in the Musée Condé collection
3 dancing angels

230 2nd century A.D. copy of the Greek work of 2nd century B.C in the public domain
at the Metropolitan Museum, New York City **3 graces**

240 from the wall painting in Babalou's Restaurant in Walnut Creek, Ca Monroe, Einstein,& Chaplin

244 3 faces eloise-ambursley-652057-unsplash .com photo by Eloise Ambursley-

256   https://commons.wikimedia.org/wiki/File:Francesco_Primaticcio_-
        _The_Three_Graces_(Aglaia,_Thalia_and_Euphrosyne).jpg   Bowes Museum
        Francesco Primaticcio (1504–1570)   Aglaia, Thalia and Euphrosyne

259A   https://commons.wikimedia.org/wiki/File:Francesco_Primaticcio_-
        _The_Three_Graces_(Aglaia,_Thalia_and_Euphrosyne).jpg   Bowers Museum

260   https://www.pikrepo.com/femke/children-playing-on-body-of-water
        License to use Creative Commons Zero - CC0

261A   https://www.pickpik.com/deer-animals-nature-wild-wildlife-forest-32627   Royalty Free Photos
        from PickPik 3 deer

261B   https://commons.wikimedia.org/wiki/File:Edgar_Degas_-_Three_Dancers_in_Red_Costume_-
        _Google_Art_Project.jpg   Edgar Degas - Three Dancers in Red Costume   Ohara Museum of Art

262   https://www.pickpik.com/lion-people-twins-sunset-nature-wild-animal-34829 two girls in from
        of lion at golden hour   Pickpic royalty free photos

263   https://www.pickpik.com/giraffe-mountain-daytime-south-africa-hluhluwe-giraffes-35474
        3 giraffes

264   https://www.pikrepo.com/fertb/three-monks-walking-on-alley-beside-statues CC0 1.0 Universal
        (CC0 1.0) three monks walking

Index

Après *Index*

*Accept the ever-shining Self-knowledge to be the only
reality. Reject all the triads, deciding them to be an
imaginary dream ... Sri Muruginar*

Here we are, out back, after the index behind the barn. Anything goes now. I would like to relate three personal experiences that have informed me.

The Blessings (1941)

Alec the *Shvatza* is the name my mother and grandmother gave him. *"Shvatza"* is Yiddish for black. Alec was an old almost baldish gray haired man with a crooked eye that came out a bit sideways. He wore an old suit jacket, crumpled baggy pants rolled at the cuffs, and large wide flat clown-like shoes. He shuffled along. At times he came to our house to wash the front porch steps. I always excited when he came to "perform this ritual." I was like his alter boy.

I would sit cross-legged at the top of the steps leaning toward him and intently watched as he worked up billows and billows of white foamy suds. So white, so beautiful! I could see his white whiskers contrasting with his dark skin. He worked hard and strong. Swish, scrub, swish, scrub as he moved the bristles of his brushes against the hard steps.

He slowed down as he was finished washing down the steps with clean water. My mother and grandmother then came back out to the porch. They would give me a packet of food and a quarter which I would reach over the steps to give to Alec. Alec would then stand up, bow slightly, and with his good eye beaming and his arms outstretched, powerfully say, "God Bless You". I remember so strongly the waves of feeling his blessing brought as it washed over me and over my mother and grandmother standing behind me.

Alec would then turn and walk his funny walk all the way down the block, turn and disappear. I only realized later that ours was the only house on the block at which Alec stopped. The memory of Alec's visits with their scrubbings, foams, and Blessing is one of my treasures.

I spent my life looking for knowledge and wisdom – at the academy and out in Asia. I forgot that everything I needed was given to me by Alec back in Baltimore at 1718 Ruxton Avenue in nineteen-forties.

The Tall Man in the Tan Suit (1944).

Three kids were playing under a table in a small room on the fifth floor of a building ancillary to the Har Zion Synagogue. Something was very funny. The kids laughed and laughed. I laughed so hard that I peed in my pants projecting two yellow streams curling across the floor from my spread-out legs. I was so embarrassed! I got out from under the table bawling, left the room, and ran down the rickety five floor staircase to the street, turned right and ran six blocks down North Avenue, crossed over, ran the two blocks down to 1718 Ruxton Avenue, burst into the house crying at the top of my lungs.

My mother cleaned me up but could not console me. She took me back up North Avenue and up to the second-floor office of the director of the day camp. He was a big man wearing a tan suit. He sat behind a large wooden desk. After hearing my mother's introduction, he pulled a chair next to his and asked me to sit. Then he posed the following scenario: "Suppose you are one of our pilots flying a Mustang engaged in a dog fight with the German Messerschmitts, flying up and down over the clouds, down into space always surrounded by the sounds of rat tat tat tat, and in the middle of this dog fight, suppose you had to pee. What would you do? You would pee in your pants and go on with the fight. And that fighter pilot would be a hero, just like you." The big man in the tan suit set me straight. I continued up more stairs and joined my friends in play. Even now, at 80 years of age, whenever I pee in my pants, I remember the tall man in the tan suit who told me I was a hero.

India (1970)

I was walking along the pilgrimage trail leading to Badrinaht, the temple at the source of the Ganges River. On the trail were wandering mendicants called sadhus, often shouting *"Badrinaht Ho"* and greeting each other with salutations of *"Rama Sita Sita Ram"* or *"Rahde Krishna Rahde"*. A week or so out on the trail we came to the confluence of the two branches of the river in the town of Devprayag. I easily moved through the town to the exact confluence in a pair of canyons though which torrents of the river gushed. All my trail companions were there singing songs in great merriment. Large steps had been carved into the rocks all the way to the water. Just above the last step a strong chain reached into the water. I held onto it as I took my dip into "Holy Mother Ganga." While I was immersed, an old man appeared out of the blue on the last step supporting the chain. He held out a handful of flower petals to me. Keeping a grip on the chain with my left hand, I reached up to receive his offering. He said *"Ananda"*. I lowered back down and I placed the flowers onto the top of the water. They turned around once or twice and sped off with the current. I came back up, dried off, saluted my trail companions and walked away from a scene which seemed 10,000 years old. In 5 minutes I came to a cigarette stand selling *beedies*, Indian cigarettes made of a single rolled tobacco leaf. The top of the stand held a large advertisement for Ganesh Beedes. The *beedies* came in a cylindrical package behind which was shown the Apollo 11 Moon landing with a similar cylindrical package. Within a 5-minute walk I gained 10 millennia. I was back in Delhi within a week staying at the apartment of the parents of my trail brother, Rahul Joshie. April heat had come and the water was turned off until 4 in the afternoon. The first bucket, thrown on the cement porch, quickly turned to steam. Each person in the house then got one bucket of water to take their bath. It was refreshing, one cup from the bucket at a time. While I was staying at the Joshie's, I read a book, <u>The Sounds of Krishna's Flute</u>,. The day before I was to leave India, Mr. Joshie told me that Kirpal Singh, author of the book, had an ashram down at the end of his block and that if I went down there, I might get his darshan. I did and was in his office with only a few other people. He told me the story of *Kaliya*, the venomous serpent with a thousand heads who poisoned the river. Krishna subdued the serpent, jumping from head to head, with the sound of his flute. Kirpal Singh told me that the serpent is the mind. As I was leaving, the guru said one last thing to me. It was the last thing I heard in my first search for wisdom in India. It had a duel meaning for me. I took it as a Zen Koan. The guru said, "And remember this, A rolling stone gathers no moss."

Appendix

During the Covid-19 of plague of 2020, David Brooks invoked Viktor Frankl's writing from "the madness of the Holocaust." (NYT 3/27/2020) "We don't get to choose our difficulties, but we do have the freedom to select our responses. Meaning, he argued, comes from three things:

- The work we offer in times of crisis
- The love we give
- Our ability to display courage in the face of suffering."

Paul Krugman writes in his column (NYT 3/27/2020) that there are three main things we should be doing to prevent the spread of the Covid-19 virus:

- We need an all-out push to get essential medical equipment to where it's needed.
- We need to slow the virus's spread by reducing personal contacts that might lead to new infections - "social distancing."
- We need to: provide financial aid to families and businesses in the face of an unavoidable economic contraction.

In 1730, New York's enslaved population reached 20 percent, prompting the New York General Assembly to issue a consolidated slave code, making it "unlawful for above three slaves" to meet on their own, and authorizing "each town" to employ "a common whipper for their slaves." (New York Times Magazine www.nytimes.com (2019/04/14 ›

"How the Pandemic Is Magnifying America's Class Divide" is an article in the "New York Times" (3/27/2020). The authors: Noam Scheiber, Nelson D. Schwartz and Tiffany Hsu point out the "pandemic caste system:

- The rich holed up in vacation properties
- The middle class marooned at home with restless children;
- The working class on the front lines of the economy, stretched to the limit by the demands of work and parenting, if there is even work to be had. "

Gaia Vince explores the human evolutionary triad in her book <u>Transcendence</u>:

- Genes
- Environment
- Culture

She writes that this "mutually reinforcing triad" is the alchemy that created our humanity. We are a species not only subject to cosmic transformations, but we are also "agents of our own transformation."

In "Scientific American," March 2020, Claudia Will wrote an article called "How Artificial Intelligence Will Change Medicine" in which a CEO said that the key to a successful AI app with its learning machine will depend on the quantity and quality of the data we feed its hungry maw. We rely on three things:

- Data
- Data
- More Data

Three aphorisms of Lester Levinson: (from his book, <u>Keys to the Ultimate Freedom</u>)

- The whole thing is simple. Any complexity in life is the ego trying to undo the simplicity of reality
- The ego will always try to keep us from letting go of the ego.
- The whole object of the path is to let go of the ego. What remains is the Self.

"Under Trump, American exceptionalism means

- Poverty,
- Misery
- Death"

is the title of the article by Robert Reich that appeared in the May 20,2020 issue of "The Guardian." He says only some of the calamity in the US is due to Trump's malfeasance but that it is due, as well, to America's longer-term failure to provide its people the basic support they need.

Three Things to Remember

A Robin Redbreast in a cage,
Puts all Heaven in a rage.

A skylark wounded on the wing
Doth make a cherub cease to sing.

He who shall hurt the little wren
Shall never be beloved by men.
By William Blake

The modern welfare state was constructed in three great waves reports the New York Times (4/9/2020):

- Progressive legislation of the early 20th century
- Roosevelt's New Deal in the 1930s
- President Johnson's Great Society, which created programs including Medicare, Medicaid and Head Start (1964 to 1965).

I had a naïve understanding of psychology in the early 1960s. I thought that there were only three psychological states:

- Psychotic
- Neurotic
- Normal

This a materialist view that doesn't understand spiritual development and the importance of love and compassion that the great jazzman, John Coltrane knew about on a 1966 tour of Japan. Coltrane was asked what he wanted to be in 10 years. "I would like to be a saint," he said. A little later, Coltrane wrote in the liner notes of his album,"A Love Supreme," "In gratitude I humbly ask to be given the means and privilege to make others happy through music." About the full expression of what it means to be human, Ken Wilber wrote, a few years later, in his book of 1973, Spectrum of Consciousness. This work was a foundational document in the field of transpersonal psychology, a discipline which takes in the full range of human psychological and spiritual experiences.

Jean Klein writes in <u>Be Who You Are</u>, "A wave which loses itself in the ocean does not lose a drop of its water. It only loses its name and form, that is, its limits; in fact, all that is negative about it. Its positive reality (water) cannot perish. Therefore what is important is neither pleasure or pain, success nor failure; what is important to understand is that neither of them have any importance whatsoever. This understanding calls for "

- Peace
- Calm
- Serenity

Google's rule of three for the way people perform their web searches:

- Go
- Know
- Do

The "go" searcher is trying to go to a particular site like the" KPFA radio station" or "The New Yorker Magazine." The "know" searcher is searching for knowledge as in "How did Charlie Parker get the nickname "Bird" or how many grains of sand are there on all the earth's beachs. The "do" seacher wants to find out how to do somethine like build a web page, brew beer, or gain enlightenment.

Please add your own triples, trios, and triads

Made in the USA
Monee, IL
13 May 2020